I Won't Read and You Can't Make Me

REACHING RELUCTANT TEEN READERS

Marilyn Reynolds

HEINEMANN
Portsmouth, NH

Heinemann
A division of Reed Elsevier Inc.
361 Hanover Street
Portsmouth, NH 03801–3912
www.heinemann.com

Offices and agents throughout the world

The author and publisher wish to thank those who have generously given permission to reprint borrowed material:

The following educators have granted permission for quotes used in the text: Sandi Moon; Lolita Pfeiffer; Carol L. Schneider; J.B. Smith, III; Sheila Konfino; and Michele A. Ritt.

"Youthful Recklessness" by Marilyn Reynolds from *English Journal,* January 1996. Copyright © 1996 by the National Council of Teachers of English, Reprinted with permission.

Library of Congress Cataloging-in-Publication Data
Reynolds, Marilyn, 1935–
    I won't read and you can't make me : reaching reluctant teen readers /
Marilyn Reynolds.
        p. cm.
    Includes bibliographical references.
    ISBN 0–325–00605–9 (alk. paper)
    1. Reading (Secondary) 2. Children with social
disabilities—Education (Secondary) 3. Motivation in education.
    I. Title.
    LB1632.R46 2004
    428.4′071′2—dc22   2003022962

Editor: Danny Miller
Production editor: Sonja S. Chapman
Cover design: Jenny Jensen Greenleaf
Compositor: QEP Design, Reuben Kantor
Manufacturing: Steve Bernier

Printed in the United States of America on acid-free paper
08 07 06 05 04 RRD   3 4 5

To the legions of teachers, librarians, aides, and administrators who work with diligence and enthusiasm to enable low-level, unmotivated, reluctant learners to join the community of lifelong readers. You are the heroes who help level the playing fields of our disenfranchised youth.

Contents

Contents

Acknowledgments

It turns out that not only does it take a village to raise a child, it takes a village to write a book. I am ever grateful to the inhabitants of my book-writing village for gifts and guidance, great and small.

My thanks to my editor, Danny Miller, for his insights, encouragement, and quirky humor—the best possible blend for getting the job done. To Carol Fifield, for inspiration and unwavering behind-the-scenes support. To Kathy Harvey, for her finely honed sense of organization and structure, her willingness to give close readings to yet one more draft, and then one more, and most of all for decades of shared highs, lows, and in-betweens along the jagged path of teaching "those" kids. To Corry Dodson, for her unfailing efficiency and good humor in pursuing and tying up myriad loose ends. To David Doty, Jeanne Lindsay, Judy Laird, and Karyn Mazo-Calf for their early enthusiasm for this project, and for close readings and comments of early drafts.

To other villagers who, perhaps unbeknownst to some, have provided fuel for the fire: Nancy Blackburn, Dan Brewer, Susan Canjura, Carla Cozart, Lynda Culp, Dale Dodson, David Doty, Renee Hamiliton, Anna Humphrey, Kathy Ikeda, Sheila Konfino, Adina Lawson, Michelle Leddell, Betsy Levine, Adele Levy, Helen Mann, Mary Lynn McMillan, John Myers, Gloria Miklowitz, Marsha Miller, Sandi Moon, Kathy Orihuela, Patty Rangel, Carol Schneider, Ellen Shimamoto, Alan Sitomer, Bitsy Wagman, and Jeannie Ward.

To Mike Reynolds, who may not have known exactly what he was getting into with his "for better or worse" vow, for his enduring love and support.

Chapter One
An Overview

*Every blade of grass has its angel that bends over
it and whispers, "grow, grow."*
From the Talmud, as quoted in *The Artist's Way*, Julia Cameron

In one of those frozen-in-time moments, on the verge of an early retirement decision, I looked fresh at the space that had, for twenty-one years, held a major substance of my days. Students, books, posters, plants, and the clutter of papers took on the quality of images collected in some ongoing picture album of my life. There was Nancy, three months earlier a poster child for the "reading sucks" contingent, lost in *Manchild in the Promised Land*. And Albert halfway through *Always Running*, the first book he'd ever tackled. A tattered *Scrabble Players Dictionary* sat crammed between *Webster's* and *The Guinness Book of World Records*, waiting for Friday's "Beat the teacher win a credit" game. Could I, should I, leave it behind?

Fate's Fickle Finger

My first position as an English teacher, in 1966, was at a new high school in Hacienda Heights, a suburb of Los Angeles. Although the term *upwardly mobile* was yet to be coined, it was essentially that kind of area, with mostly college-bound students. My schedule there included two AP sophomore classes, two regular sophomore classes, and an experimental, interdisciplinary elective class for ninth graders—team-taught with a soul mate. It was a delightful assignment and did nothing to shake my faith in well-conceived, detailed lesson plans that followed, creatively of course, the mandated curriculum. In 1969, eight months pregnant, I took a break from full-time teaching for the sake of full-time mothering.

By the time my son was three, I was ready to stick at least my big toe, if not my whole self, back into the public school teaching pool. One evening I happened to run into F, a teaching colleague of my husband's, at a market where I hardly ever shopped. I mentioned that I was hoping to find a part-time job at a public school. The next day his wife, K, who also taught high school in the same district, called to tell me of an opening for a part-time teacher at the district's alternative high school. She said the personnel department was very disorganized and the guy in charge usually hired the first woman with good legs who walked in the door. The job hadn't been "flown" yet, but if I was interested I should phone every day and be among the first interviewed. I did that for several days, always with the response that they would be scheduling interviews the next day. Then we went off to the beach for our annual family vacation.

On the Thursday morning of our first week away, we found an envelope carefully secured under the windshield wiper of our car. It was from K. They were interviewing for the job that day. If I was interested, I should drive up there first thing. "Wear a skirt," she said. Luckily I had one with me, and even though I was a strong feminist, I took K's advice.

Her note went on to say that she had heard the news of the interviews the previous evening. All she and her husband knew about where we were staying was that it was in Laguna Beach, in a house overlooking a picturesque cove. I hardly knew these folks, but they drove around Laguna, checking out cars near picturesque coves, and finally found ours.

The Demographics of Misunderstood High School

I signed a contract the afternoon of the interview, having no idea what an "alternative" school was, but happy that I could arrange my hours to fit my son's preschool schedule. The school was in another suburb of Los Angeles and was seen in that district as a school for losers—a last chance place for hoodlums, delinquents, and "knuckle draggers." Let's call the school Misunderstood High School (M.H.S.).

In truth, M.H.S. served a wide range of students, some of whom fit the stereotype and others who didn't. Some were second-generation gangbangers. Some only attended school now and then because they were babysitting younger siblings, had valid health problems, or no one was paying attention. Some had moved around so much that they'd never spent more than a semester at any one school. Some were extremely bright and some were highly challenged by even the most simple academic endeavors. Poverty, abuse, drugs, alcoholism, mental illness—every aspect of our troubled society was manifest in M.H.S.'s conglomerate student body.

The one thing our students had in common was that they were not welcome at the district's comprehensive high schools and had been shuffled through a so-called voluntary transfer process to get to us. The process was only voluntary in that, under extreme pressure and threat of total expulsion, parents and/or guardians signed their names to a form that stated they were requesting a transfer.

Some students came to M.H.S. in dread, others came willingly. Occasionally a student would request a transfer from his home school to M.H.S. The ones who *wanted* to transfer were often dissuaded from making the move. However, a student who knew she wanted to attend M.H.S. was generally savvy to the ways of working around the system. If her requested transfer was not forthcoming, she might shout the "f" word at an administrator, or light a cigarette in a classroom, thus hurrying the process along.

The whole M.H.S. student body consisted of those for whom the standard curriculum had failed repeatedly. As a result, in spite of district mandates, most teachers developed their own curriculum, materials, and methods that better suited the needs of our greatly varied assemblage.

I signed on at Misunderstood High School for the sake of convenience, knowing that in two years, when my son's schedule allowed for a longer teaching day, I would go back to a "regular" high school. But after two years at M.H.S., the only change I made was in my status from part-time to full-time teacher.

Why Stay at Misunderstood High School?

Why did I choose to stay? I was the epitome of the white middle class. Nothing in my life, or my education classes, had prepared me to deal with the unmotivated, school sucks crowd. Most of my students were of Hispanic heritage. The extent of my knowledge about their culture had to do with burritos, enchiladas, and sombreros. I hadn't even been exposed to menudo yet.

I believed that the police were not only my friend, but everyone else's friend too. Then one day I watched as a policeman slapped handcuffs on a student with such force that the student's wrist was broken. That audible crack of bone was the first crack in my naïveté regarding justice for all. The student's crime? He *looked* like someone who had robbed a convenience store.

In addition to the myriad troubles besetting M.H.S. students, there was also an abundance of resiliency and hope. To be part of a "loser's" successful journey toward high school graduation, or respectable employment, or personal stability, was addictive. And even though my students and I came from totally different backgrounds, we somehow, mostly, managed to connect and, in the connecting, to educate one another. Perhaps I stayed because of the angel bending over me whispering "grow, grow." Was it that same whispering voice that guided me to the market where I happened to see F? Or was our meeting just another of those lucky serendipitous events that come out of nowhere but end up leading somewhere?

The Gift of a Reading Habit

Over time I came to realize that the greatest gift I could offer my students, many of whom would have no further formal schooling after they left M.H.S., was the gift of a reading habit. Silent reading time became the backbone of my program. Encouraging and developing a reading habit in M.H.S.'s reluctant readers was the task to which I devoted most of my teaching energies. It was a task in which I believed wholeheartedly, except . . .

There were those district-level department meetings with *real* English teachers from *real* high schools. They couldn't possibly offer independent reading time at the expense of "Julius Caesar." And the ninth-grade teachers! They didn't have time to do *anything* but grammar! That was where the foundation was laid for all future writing. Their students would never learn comma usage if they didn't know their appositives!

Although I considered myself to be a good writer, I had not yet had anything published, and I lacked the courage to stand before my peers and say with certainty that I couldn't tell an appositive from an appetizer, yet my comma usage was consistently error free.

I would leave a meeting of district English teachers feeling that perhaps I was doing my students an injustice by not pounding in grammar and the classics. Maybe I was lazy because I wasn't turning myself inside out putting on highly motivating one-woman dramatic productions of "Julius Caesar." Was I simply self-indulgent because I spent part of my own classroom time reading for pleasure?

As convinced as I was of the overriding importance of leading students to a reading habit, I lacked the confidence needed to spread the word to my English teacher colleagues because I was without the basics of theory and research needed to support my intuitive approach to teaching.

Gaining Credibility and Consciousness

Finally, I had the opportunity and good sense to pursue a master's degree. In 1981, I received an M.S. in Reading Education from Pepperdine University. The work I did during the course of that degree was challenging both academically and professionally—forcing me to evaluate my own teaching practices in the larger context of a cohesive teaching/learning theory.

My practice during that first decade at M.H.S. had been simply to require that each day students read something that held meaning for them, and that they write something of meaning in their daily journals. Yes, we occasionally watched a movie. We frequently engaged in a degree of spontaneous group discussion. There was the occasional "beat the teacher" Scrabble game. Generally though, it was "read something *you* choose, and write something that comes from *your* heart."

The Pepperdine work helped me evaluate and modify what was effective and what was left wanting in my fly-by-the-seat-of-the-pants methods, and it also, both on a district level and in my own personal reflections, gave credibility to my classroom practices. I added significantly to my repertoire of techniques to help low-level readers and continued to direct my teaching energies toward guiding students to books and activities that would be meaningful to them.

Reading for Life

Several years ago the *Los Angeles Times* reported on the findings of a research study that showed the single most significant factor in determining a person's success in life to be whether they read for pleasure. *That* they read was important—*what* they read was not. The study's focus on success included not only the obvious, in work and career, but also success in family and interpersonal relations and in an enhanced sense of satisfaction with life in general.

The transfer from classroom experiences to real life is often not apparent. Yet isn't that why we work so hard to educate our youth? To better prepare them for life? What better preparation can we offer than a "reading for life" classroom, where student activities mimic those of adults who read for pleasure?

With continued emphasis on reading something of one's own choosing, my ongoing frustration was in finding the right book for the right student. A significant number of students could get caught by *The Outsiders* and *Go Ask Alice*. Books by Judy Blume often appealed to the nonmotivated girls.

L.A. county juvenile hall must have had hundreds of copies of *Down These Mean Streets* and *The Cross and the Switchblade* because boys newly released from "juvie," where they'd started but not finished such a book, often requested these titles. But after the limited tried-and-true choices, then what?

Except for the rare avid reader who entered my realm, complete with an interest in certain classics, or medical thrillers, or spy novels, or sci-fi, students entered M.H.S. convinced that reading was boring and stupid. We desperately needed hundreds more books with which our at-risk students could connect. More out of desperation than ambition, I decided to try my hand at writing such a book.

The Fusion of Teaching and Writing

In 1989, my first teen novel, *Telling*, was published. It is the story of a twelve-year-old girl who is being molested by a neighbor. It took nine months to write. Two years and twenty-two rejections later, it got published. I'm sure I would have given up after the first ten or so rejections if it had not been for my student readers. I had a copy of the three-inch-thick manuscript, in a green three-holed binder, sitting on a table in my classroom. Slowly, unbelievingly, I noticed that several students were making it a point to get to class early to get the manuscript. I spent a significant portion of my next paycheck at Kinkos, getting five more manuscript copies for classroom use, bought another $120 worth of postage stamps, and kept sending the manuscript out.

Another vacancy on my bookshelves was waiting for a realistic teen pregnancy novel. *Detour for Emmy* was my next book, and I found that the second book was much easier to get published than the first. After Emmy's story, I took on *Too Soon for Jeff*—teen pregnancy from a boy's viewpoint. I wrote two and a half books while teaching full time, but the necessary juggling act was not an easy one. If my husband and I went to a movie on the weekend, I felt guilty because it meant I wouldn't complete Chapter 4 as planned. And if I skipped the movie and completed Chapter 4, I was plagued by guilt because my husband was getting short shrift.

Halfway through *Too Soon for Jeff*, writing this time with a contract and an advance, I decided to take to heart another adage from *The Artist's Way*, "Leap, and the net will appear." I'm nothing if not practical, and this is not an adage that I keep in mind when walking across bridges or standing near fourteenth-floor windows, but it was a very useful metaphor as I struggled with the "could I, should I" early retirement decision.

From Teacher/Writer to Writer/Teacher

I took one of those deals in which I would continue to teach twenty-five days out of the school year for a period of five years. This would supplement my meager retirement allowance, and, since I was writing realistic teen fiction, it would keep me in touch with my reading audience. From being a teacher/writer I became a writer/teacher and set about finishing book number three.

During the first writing year, somewhere in the middle of rewriting a paragraph, I sat at my computer in my home office, gazing out the window at squirrels stealing bird food and laughing at our dog frantically jumping to reach the never reachable squirrel, and contemplated my new life. Even though I'd not been the sort of teacher you would ever see on TV proudly holding high a "Best Teacher of the Year" trophy, I had touched lives. I had been part of some amazing "turn-around" stories. And, as much as I reveled in the writing time, I missed the thrill of the "this is the first book I ever read" experiences. I missed the daily contact with the wildly varied assortment of last chancers, and I wondered what I was doing with my life. But then the letters and, later, emails came my way.

I Get Letters

Hello Marilyn Reynolds! I have read all of your novels. . . . These books helped me realize that I don't want to be a fourteen-year-old mother. Right now I just want to take care of myself and finish school. Thank you.   Betty P.

I just finished reading But What About Me? *and it was the most touching book I ever read. I'm a guy but I can feel for her. Thank you.*   S.V.

I really enjoy reading your books. . . . They have helped me grow and be strong. And I know I'm not alone in the world. . . .   Caila M.

> *Your books have turned non-readers into insatiable readers as well as having opened up areas for sensitive discussion. Your books have made life "okay" for some of my girls who have discovered their own personal situations in the books they are reading. You need to know how much I/we appreciate your work. . . .   Sandi Moon, a teacher*

Such letters continue to thrill me and to remind me that, through my books, I am still an instrument in the process of leading reluctant readers to a lifelong reading habit. That awareness comforts me when I'm indulgently sipping coffee and watching the squirrels when you, my colleagues, are quite often swimming upstream against the current of education trends, working to bring meaningful education into the lives of so many desperately at-risk teens.

I now have eight books of teen fiction in the True-to-Life from Hamilton High Series. Several personal essays have been published in newspapers or anthologies. School visits, teacher workshops, and conferences all serve to keep me in touch with the broader worlds of teens and teachers, and for that I am grateful. There are, in truth, only so many hours of squirrel watching and rewriting that same old paragraph that I can stand.

Teach to True Standards

If you are buried in the muck and mire of mandates, it helps to remember that the practice of Sustained Silent Reading unquestionably leads to improved skills. But the essence of such reading has to do with the increased understanding of one's self and of the world, of enabling the wounded to heal, the isolated to know they are not alone, the bigoted to see the humanity of others. It is about helping the disconnected connect with the world beyond them, and the world within them. These are the standards by which all curriculum and learning activities should be measured.

Practical Information on What's to Come

Sustained Silent Reading, or SSR, is mentioned throughout this book. Unfortunately, there are situations in which SSR has taken on a "Shut Up and Read" attitude, where teachers offer a reading model but do not offer much in the way of guidance for book choices, variety of books, or positive troubleshooting efforts when reading bogs down. As a result, some teachers believe the SSR designation is tainted, and they prefer the term *independent reading* to describe what others of us call SSR. I've chosen to stay with the Sustained Silent Reading label because it is more widely used and defined. But I'm talking about a program that goes far beyond a Shut Up and Read approach. I'm talking about a program that can lead low-level reluctant readers along the path to a lifelong reading habit—a "reading for life" program.

Tricks of the Trade

Throughout *I Won't Read and You Can't Make Me* various forms, ideas, and techniques that will be useful for a Sustained Silent Reading program are mentioned. The Tricks of the Trade section identified by the letters TOTT in parentheses within the text and by the magic hat in the margin, offers further explanation and specific forms that may be copied for classroom use.

READERS ASK

Dear Ms. R,

How can I find any time for SSR when I must spend so much time preparing my students for standardized tests?

Teaching As Fast As I Can

Dear Speedy,

Take heart. Combined with other directed activities, SSR *is* teaching to the test. Sheila Konfino, who teaches teen parents at the Seaford Avenue School in Long Island, NY, reports that her previously reluctant readers have become avid readers through the True-to-Life from Hamilton High Series: "We are starting to see the impact reading has had on improving their skills. Over 92 percent of TAP's (Teenage Parenting Program) eleventh graders successfully passed the New York State Comprehensive English Language Arts examination in January . . . an outstanding achievement."

For Sheila's students, the Hamilton High books were "hits." She reports that "perhaps one of the greatest moments of my teaching career was when a fifteen-year-old pregnant student came to me with tears in her eyes and told me that she was so proud of herself because it was the first time in her life that she had ever finished reading a whole book. She asked me if I had any more books for her to read. This was my dream come true!"

The importance of this story is not that *my* series turns reluctant readers around, it is that *any* book a student connects with can change his or her life. Through SSR you *are* teaching to the test, but best of all, you're offering your students the transforming gift of a lifelong reading habit.

M.R.

Questions Only You Can Answer

○ Are my students engaged in activities that hold meaning for them?

○ How can I tie silent reading time to my district's mandated curriculum?

○ Is there something in my district or state standards that mentions turning out "lifelong learners" as a major objective?

○ In establishing or continuing an SSR program, who on the staff and faculty at my school are my allies?

Chapter Two
I Won't Read and You Can't Make Me

The common reader . . . differs from the critic and the scholar. He is worse educated, and nature has not gifted him so generously. He reads for his own pleasure rather than to impart knowledge or correct the opinions of others. Above all, he is guided by an instinct to create for himself, out of whatever odds and ends he can come by, some kind of whole.

The Common Reader, Virginia Woolf

The Challenge of an Outspoken Reluctant Reader

On Nancy's first day in my English classroom at M.H.S., she announced to me: "I won't read and you can't make me."

"Won't or can't?" I asked.

"Won't!" She hated to read, had never read a book, and never would. Plenty of teachers had tried, she'd said, lifting herself to her full five feet ten inches and looking down on me defiantly.

Only Anna looked up from *Go Ask Alice* to observe the new student and our interaction. The other twelve, sitting at library-style tables or curled up in bean-bag chairs, remained engrossed in their books.

There was Julio, his head bent low over the table, *The Lion, the Witch and the Wardrobe* resting on his knees. He was visiting Narnia, forgetting for the moment the burden of heavy black stylized letters tattooed across the back of his neck, broadcasting his gang loyalty.

There was Maria, reading *Breaking Free From Partner Abuse*, a book I fervently hoped would guide her toward a better path than the one she was on. *Manchild in the Promised Land*, *Always Running*, *The Guinness Book of World Records*, *The Picture Book of Dog Breeds Around the World*, *The Color Purple*, *Forever*, and a variety of other subjects and stories were gripping this ragtag group of high schoolers.

Simple Requirements for English Credit

Nancy's "I won't read" remarks were prompted by a one-sheet handout I gave each student on his or her first day of class. It outlined how to get English credit in my classes.

1. Read independently from a book of your choice each day.
2. Write briefly in your Reading Log (TOTT, pp. 86–91).
3. Write at least one page in your journal on a topic of your choice.

The handout offered more details, but those three requirements are the essentials.

"Why do you think I'll try to make you read?" I asked the puffed up Nancy.

She pointed to number one on the handout.

"So . . . you *read* that?"

Anna smiled, and Julio left Narnia for a moment.

Nancy spoke to me in a slow, deliberate tone, much like the tone my mother had always used when she was losing patience with me: "*Books. I— won't— read— books. You–can't–make–me–read–a— book.*"

I expected her to call me "Marilyn Ann," or "young lady," at any moment.

Nancy found a place to sit and I gave her a folder, complete with log sheet, and a journal notebook of the ten-cent, bought-in-bulk variety. She filled out a Reading Questionnaire (TOTT, pp. 92–95) and brought it to my desk. Her answers were predictable: She wasn't read to as a child. She'd never read a book. Reading was boring and a waste of time.

Journals

I always read journals (TOTT, pp. 96–100) at the end of the day. This was partly because I didn't want work piling up to the extent that I would have to take it home, but mainly because of a frightening experience I'd had a few years back. I'd gone three days without reading journals, and when I began the "catch-up" task, I read a student entry in which he was questioning whether life was worth living. Three days had passed, and he'd not been in school since he'd written of his despair. A quick phone call reassured me that my student was still among the living, and the follow-up process began. But that was the last time journals went unread at the end of the day.

Because our classes were limited to twenty, and because average daily attendance ran somewhere between 60 and 70 percent, journal reading was not a burdensome task. My comments and questions were brief, sometimes just a check mark to let the student know I'd read the work.

Nancy's journal on her first day of class was a repeat in writing of what she'd already indicated. She hated reading, would not read, it was a waste of time. School was a waste of time, but her grandmother had convinced her that she could get a better job if she had a high school diploma. She wanted to get the necessary credits, fast, and "get the fuck out."

Foul Language

Unlike some of the other "I hate to read" students, Nancy's writing was neat and error free. The beginnings of her sentences were capitalized, and she knew where to put periods and commas. There were no spelling errors.

I did not react to the "f" word. "F you" would win a quick suspension, but the generalized adjective, noun, verb variations slid by with the ease of a misplaced modifier. "Fuck," "shit," "asshole," and hundreds of others were examples of many students' home vocabulary—their first language. To attack that too early was to put up barriers that would block more important goals.

I glanced over at Nancy as she opened her journal. "Nice writing," I had commented in the margin of her first journal entry.

Nancy gave me a look, then turned the page in her journal, wrote the date, and waited.

Although Nancy stubbornly refused to read, she did write in her journal. First though, we had to go through a certain ritual.

Nancy's Journal-Writing Ritual

"What can I write about?"

"Anything you want to write about."

"I can't think of anything."

"Write what's on your mind."

"Nothing's on my mind."

"Then choose from one of the topics on the board." Every day, under the heading of "If you're stumped for writing ideas," I wrote three possibilities (TOTT, pp. 99–100): "What's one of your earliest memories?" "Write about a time when you were very frightened." "What did you do last weekend?"

Nancy perused the topics. "Do I have to write about that stupid stuff?"

"No. Write about anything you want."

"But what if I can't think of anything?"

"Then write *that!*"

When Nancy finally got around to putting pen to paper, she occasionally mentioned her grandmother, but mostly she wrote about how stupid school was—every school she'd ever been to (she listed fifteen) was stupid, but this school was the most stupid of all: The teachers were stupid; the kids were stupid; the guy with the tattoo on his neck was *really* stupid; and, worst of all, the school smelled like *shit!*

She was right about the stench. Between our classroom and the science room was a yard space only about 20 by 15 feet. In that space, as part of various science projects, there was a goat, two sheep, chickens, ducks, rabbits, and two tortoises. It sent up a constant and pervasive stink that defied air fresheners.

Finally, a "Hit" Book for Nancy

Each day during reading time I placed two or three books on the table in front of Nancy—*Flowers in the Attic*, a Danielle Steele book or two, *Are You There God, It's Me, Margaret*, *No One Here Gets Out Alive*. Nothing worked. She thumbed through them, then shoved them aside.

"I told you I won't read books," she sometimes reminded me as I plunked other possibilities down in front of her.

"Yes, you did, but you also told me you wanted to earn English credit, fast."

And so it went.

The most credible recommendations for books come from other students. When Anna finished *Go Ask Alice*, she said to Nancy, "This is a really good book." Finally, after two long and tedious weeks of perfunctory glances at books I'd placed in front of her, repetitions of her "I won't read" stance, and arguments over why she never got full credit for a day's work, she took Anna's recommendation, got caught by *Go Ask Alice*, read it in a week, and demanded another book just like that one. I handed her a second copy of *Go Ask Alice*. She slammed it down on the table.

In a tone bordering on affection, she muttered, "Fuckin' Reynolds."

Gramma Gets the Point

I then set *Rubyfruit Jungle* in front of her. She opened it cautiously, as if it had been sitting in the muck of the stench-filled adjoining pen. But she read it all period, then asked to take it home.

The first chapter of *Rubyfruit Jungle* is one of the funniest and most poignant eight pages ever written. It seems to me as innocent as playing doctor, but not everyone agrees with my assessment.

Here's how it goes. When eight-year-old Molly accepts her cousin's, Broccoli Detweiler's, invitation to "watch me take a leak," she is shocked by the look of his uncircumcised penis, but also hears opportunity knocking. She tells Broc:

"No one else has a dick like that. I bet you got the only one in the world. We oughta make some money off it."

"Money? How we gonna make money off my dick?"

"After school we can take the kids back here [at the edge of the woods] and show you off, and we charge a nickel apiece."

"No. I ain't showing people my thing if they're gonna laugh at it."

"Look, Broc, money is money. What do you care if they laugh? You'll have money then you can laugh at them. And we split it fifty-fifty."

There follows another three or four pages about Molly and Broc's business venture, then their teacher learns what they're doing and things take a turn.

Nancy read those pages to her grandmother that evening.

The next day, Nancy came marching into class, waving her book at me. "My gramma said she didn't know if I should be reading this book or not."

"What did you say?"

"I told her we read real shit at M.H.S., not like that *fake* shit you're supposed to read at *fakie* Washington High School."

"And . . . ?"

"And she said it was good to see me with my nose in a book, so maybe it was okay."

Nancy Spreads the News

Nancy quickly became a hungry reader, demanding a book "just like this one" as she handed in one extra credit book report after another. She soon became the class spokesperson for the joy of reading.

A month or so after Nancy's transformation, she overheard Gabriel, a new student, saying he didn't like to read.

"Dude," she said. "That's how I used to be, but check it out, there're *real* books here." She handed him a copy of *Always Running*, exactly the book I would have shown him.

Gabriel looked at her as if she were crazy, but he took the book from her. I gave him the credit information sheet, a folder, and a journal, and he took them to a table at the far corner where he sat facing the door—where most new students chose to sit. After the class settled in I would explain more thoroughly the details of earning English credit in my class. But by then Gabriel was engrossed in *Always Running,* so I decided our talk could wait a day.

At the end of class, Nancy walked past Gabriel on her way to the folder box. "Told you," she said.

He gave her a nod—meaning what? I was never quite sure what the nods meant. But she smiled, and when he came to class the next day, he asked for that "running" book. Gabriel was a much easier sell on the joys of reading than Nancy had been, but then Nancy herself had done the sales pitch for Gabriel.

READERS ASK

Dear Ms. R,

What can I do when my "hate to read" students don't come around as easily as your Nancy did?

Ms. Wondering

Dear Wondering,

Nancy didn't seem easy at the time, even though the whole process was only a matter of weeks. If there is a very broad range of books to choose from, and if you guide your "hate to read" (HTR) students to books based on what you know about their interests, eventually most students will come to appreciate reading. Sometimes, though, it takes a looooonnnnnggggg time. Keep offering books of all kinds to the HTRs. Pay attention to their questionnaires. Talk with them about their interests. Keep trying, and know that your chances are very good that somewhere along the way you and HTRs will find that "hit" book that opens the reading door.

Of course, I would go ridiculously far beyond Pollyanna if I claimed that eventually every HTR kid will come around. In Chapter 7, you'll read the story of Herman who is only one example of many who never climbed on the reading bandwagon. With the Hermans, use every possible resource to reach them, or to move them to another class or program where they *may* be reached. In the meantime, Hermans don't get to disturb other readers.

M.R.

Dear Ms. R,

Why should I allow foul language in my classroom? Shouldn't they be learning to speak properly? They'll never get jobs if every other word is offensive to decent society.

Fed up with f—

Dear Fed,

As teachers, we have to honor our own standards when making decisions regarding what behavior and language is appropriate in our classrooms. If you need a strict "no foul language" policy in your classroom, my advice would be for you to stick with that.

I grew up during a time when the "f" word caused women to faint, or at least reach for the smelling salts, and was at first shocked to hear the language of my at-risk students. When I decided early on to let their "f—s" and "sh—s" pass as modifiers, it was because I simply wasn't ready to attack their home language before we had developed a mutual sense of respect.

M.R.

Questions Only You Can Answer

❍ What's going on with my least willing reader?

❍ Is she unable to read fluently enough to enjoy a book?

❍ Is something going on in his life that keeps his mind so occupied that he can think of nothing else?

❍ Might she need glasses?

❍ Would it be helpful for me to talk with the counselor or nurse about this student (assuming your school has such support people)?

❍ How do I keep my frustration with the unwilling reader from turning to anger?

❍ How do I not lose hope?

Chapter Three

Let Me Tell You This,
Reading Will Lead Lives

Every child, and the child in every one of us, is ready to plead:
Tell me a story. For the role of stories is to explain life, and
the good stories, in their very substance and in the structure
of their language, become revelation.

Our Lady of the Lost and Found, Diane Schoemperlen

José Appreciates the Value of Reading

I sometimes get letters asking what my next book will be, urging me to hurry up.
Awhile back I got such a letter from José, a young man in a youth facility in Texas.
I answered, confessing that I was not working on another novel, but instead was

working on a book about helping reluctant readers develop reading habits. He wrote back, expressing his disappointment that I didn't have another novel on the way. But then he added a P.S.:

> Let me tell you this. When I first came to San Saba I didn't know how to read, speak and write English as much as I do now. Reading will lead lives.

The Reading for Pleasure and Improved Writing Skills Connection

The first letter I received from José was two years previous to the "Reading will lead lives" message. He said he had just finished reading *Telling*, the first book he'd ever read, and wanted to know how to get more of my books. His letter consisted of sixty mostly misspelled words and his print was large, like that of a primary student. Seven letters and two years later, his missive was more than 250 words, written on narrow-lined paper. He offered specific, sophisticated comments about *Love Rules*, and he asked for advice on a writing project he wanted to start. He told me, "Your books are a blessing to people like me" and said that reading helps him think about his life.

The latest envelope from José is ten pages, both sides—the beginning of his own story. He has an important story to tell and he's intent on telling it. He is now quite articulate in spite of a wealth of "mechanical" errors. His acknowledgments indicate his generous spirit:

> His parents, "who are loving and caring for my future, and most important, my relationship with God."
>
> Marilyn Reynolds for "encouraging me to face reality and not just back off the facts of the struggles of life. And to understand the power of the human spirit."
>
> His ESL teacher who "helped me with my daily schoolwork and gave me the chance to practice my beautiful Spanish language."
>
> His librarian, who "I want to appreciate for helping me to continue to stay focused on my reading, and for her good sense of humor."

He also acknowledged several others who offered him help and encouragement along the way.

I don't know why José is locked up, nor do I know if the insights he has gained over the past few years will be enough to carry him when he has to make it on his own. The difficulties of finding work with a criminal record, of finding affordable housing, and of living on the edge of poverty may be next to impossible for him. Will his old familiar life draw him back? The realist in me knows the odds, but the idealist believes he has a fighting chance and that his reading habit may help carry him beyond predictability.

Reading for Pleasure Opens Closed Minds

Another striking "reading will lead lives" story came to me several years ago. A Michigan teacher wrote that some of her alternative school students were "neo-Nazi, Michigan militia-type, white, homophobic, rural and suburban, fifteen to twenty year olds." Knowing I taught reading at an alternative high school, she asked if I might send her a list of "poignant, hard-hitting books which demonstrate overcoming obstacles." She explained that fiction was the only way she could get some of her hard-core students to confront life issues.

She went on to tell me of one of her skinhead males who had never read a whole book before he read *Too Soon for Jeff*. This was "a very anti-Semitic person who refused to participate in class discussion regarding discrimination and prejudice . . ."

After her student read *Too Soon for Jeff*, he felt he could be successful at reading another book, so, at his teacher's recommendation, he read Elie Weisel's *Night*. This is a horrific story based on Weisel's own experiences in Birkenau, Auschwitz, and Buchenward, and it began Wiesel's lifelong mission to bear witness for those who died in the Holocaust.

The beginning of a dramatic turnaround in this previously non-reading student was evidenced in his report when he wrote: "I admire the strength of Jewish people. . . . I never knew Jews were such good people."

More such "reading leads lives" examples came recently when a long-time teacher friend of mine decided to use *Love Rules* in her community college classroom. Her students were mostly second-year education majors—a mix of Hmong, Mexican, black, white—and they were generally from cultures that do not openly discuss sex, much less homosexuality. *Love Rules* deals with a friendship between two high school senior girls, one straight and one lesbian, with the put-downs and bullying that occur as the lesbian girl becomes more obvious about her gender identity.

At the end of the semester, the students' notes my teacher friend forwarded to me included:

I am mad at my friends because some of them are just like the jokes.

I don't think I can change what my family feels about people who are gay but from now on *I* will be more understanding.

Thanks for writing about people like me and my partner.

Books—A Place to Be When One's Own World Is Toxic

Marta was undoubtedly one of the brightest and most talented students ever to cross the threshold of Room 9, and she was also one of the most troubled. The last time I'd seen her she was being led away from school, handcuffed, having been caught in the girls' room shooting heroin into a vein between her toes. For years she had been prostituting herself for the sake of her habit.

Nearly four years after I'd witnessed that sad scene a letter from Marta arrived at my home address. She wrote reminding me of the variety of books she'd read while enrolled in my class—Hawthorne and Melville, Anaïs Nin and Virginia Wolfe, *The Story of Sid and Nancy*, also *Sybil* and *Portrait of a Marriage* by Nigel Nicolson and Vita Sackville-West, to mention only a few.

She said that she was out of rehab, working in a bookstore, getting her life together. She thanked me for providing books, and "a place I could be when I couldn't be in the world." Through all of her troubles, she never stopped reading.

Reading Toward Healing and Wholeness

One of my colleagues once lightened the mood of a faculty meeting by saying:

> If I were to suffer a heart attack during sixth period, I trust that Marilyn would call 911 and perform CPR until the paramedics arrived. But by the time they were carrying me out the door, she would have placed that Norman Cousins book, *The Healing Heart*, on the stretcher beside me. I *think* it would be in that order, emergency procedures first and then the book, but . . . ?

In spite of my reputation, I have no illusion that one need only hand a person a book and she can kick a heroin habit, or that the right book can turn a sociopath into a philanthropist, or that reading can conquer a heart attack.

Adolph Hitler and Timothy McVeigh were avid readers, as is Charles Manson. Reading can't do it all. But for most of us, and for most of our students, reading can be a very important part of a journey toward wholeness, or health, or enlightenment, or whatever label we attach to the mystery of intellectual and spiritual growth.

Our job as teachers is to find books that will capture student readers—give them a jump-start on their reading journeys. This means having an abundance of raw, in-your-face books, books about the pain and suffering of drugs, gangs, and abuse of all sorts. This is one of the hardest parts: trust the choice of the developing reader, and be brave in book selections. However, it is crucial that we make such books available, that we not take the safe route of only placing materials on our shelves that could not possibly offend anyone.

READERS ASK

Dear Ms. R,

How can I possibly find a "hit" book for the boy who thinks reading is boring and stupid, and not so subtly implies I am too?

How can I reach the girl who wants to spend the whole SSR time putting on makeup? And why shouldn't she, because "we're not doing anything, anyway."

Tired of teaching airheads and hoodlums

Dear Tired,

The best way to capture the blatantly reluctant reader is to have a huge variety of books on your shelves. It's good to have some shockers—things they think you might be too boring to choose—such as books with colorful pictures of body piercings and tattoos. Skateboarding books. Books depicting the most disgusting rap artists you can imagine. Let them know by your book collection that you're a person open to many tastes, and that you can respect their taste in books also.

One teacher from a highly successful SSR program advises keeping a large selection of glossy books with plenty of pictures—books of wild animals, cities, horses and dogs, and disasters. Very low-level readers may not be ready to tackle a chapter book, but pictures draw them in. Their curiosity leads them to the text.

Action, adventure, sports, schlocky romances, survival stories, mysteries, any genre, any reading level, should all be well represented on your shelves. The Mirrors of the Soul—Windows to Others booklist (TOTT, pp. 115–120) includes many M.H.S. "hit" books. The others have been highly recommended by teachers of reluctant readers, or by students.

In reviewing the list for this book, I was very tempted to remove *Sybil*, *Dibs in Search of Self*, and a number of others that are complex and seemingly difficult reading for low-level readers. But for each title I questioned, an image arose of an unlikely reader glued to the book, and my little finger refused to reach for the delete key.

M.R.

Dear Ms. R,

How can I possibly accumulate a wide range of books for my classroom library? I'm in three different classrooms every day.

No Place to Call Home

Dear Homeless,

Isn't that just the biggest pain in the derrière? One thing you might do is to divide your classroom library between the three places so that you have several interesting choices in each classroom. Of course, when Roshann finishes the first book she's ever read and wants another one right now, the book you *know* will be perfect for her is in the room you just left. Depending on how much wiggle room there is in your respective schedules, she might pick it up from you at lunchtime or after school. Maybe you'll need to bring it to her the next day.

A rolling cart filled with a variety of books will help you with your library system. Exchange several of these books each day so that students have the opportunity to choose from all of your titles rather than just from the one-third in each of your classrooms.

Finally, if you can do so without losing your integrity, become *very* good friends with whatever administrator/clerk works out the room assignments.

M.R.

Dear Ms. R,

There is very little money in our school budget for books other than textbooks, which my reluctant readers don't even want to lift, much less read. What to do?

Might Become a Coach

Dear Might,

Ideally your district would so value SSR that dollars galore would be budgeted for paperback books. However, since you're apparently not teaching in Paradise, you might consider the annual book sale at the largest library near you. See if the library will take a purchase order, or if you can, get a petty cash check to take with you; the piddling amount of money allotted for books will go much farther this way. Also used bookstores are a source of inexpensive books.

Donations of books from parents and other teachers are sometimes more trouble than they're worth. Do you really need to find a place on your shelves for a 1982 physics textbook that someone has finally decided to part with? In this case, it is definitely the thought that counts, and it's a valuable thought—a parent has at least considered the possibility that the school needs more books.

I once received eighty-two Silhouette romances from a well-meaning mother. With my "let them read pap and drivel" attitude, I was not against having Silhouettes on the shelves, but eighty-two? I kept a few and took the rest to a used bookstore where they gave me credit toward other books. Nearly always such stores will have a few copies of *Catcher in the Rye* or *Rubyfruit Jungle*. Usually, there is an abundance of John Grisham, Tom Clancy, Dean Koontz, Danielle Steele, Stephen King, and other popular best sellers, so donated trade-ins can be of use.

Orders for books that include the latest Young Adult (YA) hits, and other current releases, probably must go through the standard, slow-moving bureaucratic channels. And . . . there's that money issue again. For the long haul, start working on shifting the balance of your school's budget. Enlist the help of other like-minded teachers. Present the most supportive power of the powers that be with your suggestions for a minor budget shift.

I'm guessing your plate is already full to the brim without adding grant writing to the heap. But if you're willing, money can be found for books through grants. Get help from the district-level person who works with grants and should know what's available to fit your needs.

Service clubs and businesses are often quite eager to support local education programs once a need is brought to their attention. Arrange to make a brief presentation about your program. This is especially effective if you take a few students who are willing to proclaim their newfound love of reading through SSR. Even if they only donate $150, that can go a long way at a library sale.

For a while I taught in a book-buying paradise where I had access to a petty cash fund. If I saw a book at a conference or store that I was sure would work with my students, I bought it, took in a receipt, and was quickly reimbursed. Eventually, someone on a district level got word that M.H.S. had a very simple and efficient way of buying books, so petty cash book buying was immediately abolished.

The next best thing to petty cash is to have an open purchase order at a nearby bookstore. This doesn't do anything for you when you're at the Monterey Aquarium and find an amazingly beautiful picture book on the life of otters, an animal that the non-reading Leticia is nearly obsessed with. But it does give you a place to run to when you suddenly notice there are no more copies of *Holes* on your shelves.

M.R.

Dear Ms. R,

My most popular books have a tendency to walk away. How can I keep from losing so many books?

Diminishing Returns

Dear Diminishing,

This is a dilemma, but one that's best treated with a degree of philosophical acceptance. Of course you have a checkout system, and you take reasonable precautions to ensure that books checked out get returned. But a book might be left at Dad's on a weekend stay, and Dad might suddenly, and without notice, move back to Texas. Or if it's a "hit" book, students may pass it on to a friend, or to someone else in the family. The possibilities are endless. Think of it this way. If the unreturned book ends up being passed around and read and talked about, it is an education dollar very well spent.

We *do* have the choice of never losing a book, but it's not a wise choice. I once taught with an extremely conscientious teacher who kept his classroom library in two locked cupboards. Students could not see or browse through the books without being carefully monitored by him. He did not let books leave his classroom. During a time when we had a schoolwide SSR program, he complained constantly that his students wouldn't read. During SSR time, most of his students did worksheets because "it keeps them quiet." Needless to say, he was not maintaining a "reading for life" classroom. But *you* are, and you'll lose books along the way, and you must try not to lose sleep over it. You also must replace the lost titles quickly because they are most likely the books that teens connect with, that feed their souls.

M.R.

Questions Only You Can Answer

○ What was *your* first "hit" book?

○ What books have changed your way of thinking, inspired you, or brought you great pleasure? Might you share a bit of that experience and read a short passage to your class?

○ How can you reach the reluctant and/or hostile student? Might a book of "Far Side" cartoons break the ice?

Chapter Four

Do You Ever Get in Trouble for Using Bad Words in Your Books?

It's not just the books under fire now that worry me. It is the books that will never be written. The books that will never be read. And all due to the fear of censorship. As always, young readers will be the real losers.

Places I Never Meant to Be, Judy Blume

No Bad Words

During a school visit to La Puente High School in La Puente, California, an earnest reader asked: "Do you ever get in trouble for using bad words in your books?"

The dog trainer's mantra is, "There are no bad dogs, only bad dog owners." As a word lover, my equivalent mantra is, "There are no bad words, only bad word users." Many words are inappropriate in the classroom, or sitting next to one's sweet old auntie at a family celebration, but the same words may be quite appropriate, even necessary, in other situations. I write realistic teen fiction, and the realities of teen life sometimes include bad words. My books are sometimes challenged and, on rare occasions, the censors prevail. Whether that constitutes "getting into trouble," I'm not sure. But I am certain beyond a doubt that censorship is trouble.

Realism Is Necessary in a Molestation Story

When I first sat down to write *Telling*, I knew that I wanted the book to offer some clarity and insight into the pervasive problem of child molestation. Most preteens and up have a fairly clear definition of rape. But what about the trusted family friend, the one she's known since she was a baby, who now has his hands places she'd rather he not? Or the uncle who holds her too tightly on his lap and rubs forcefully against her?

The National Resource Council states that the largest retrospective study on the prevalence of child sexual abuse found 27 percent of women and 16 percent of men reported they had been abused—roughly one out of three girls and one out of six boys.

The problem crosses all boundaries of economic classes, levels of education, and racial/ethnic backgrounds, and it resides in a gray area that often leaves its victims confused and silent. If *Telling* were to add clarity, it would have to include realistic scenes. For example, I couldn't write, "Fred Sloane did some things that made me very uncomfortable, but I didn't know how to talk about them," when I needed to write:

> He [Fred Sloane] backed me against the garage and leaned his whole body hard against me. . . . He pushed my head back with his hand, holding my chin tight. He put his mouth, open, over mine. It was sloppy wet and tasted of popcorn—salty and greasy and stale.
>
> "You're getting to be quite a babe, you know? These cute little bumps are getting bigger," he said, brushing his hand across my chest. . . . Don't worry, you won't lose your cherry. We'll just have a little fun . . .
>
> I knew something was wrong. . . . I knew it was something dirty because it felt dirty. I thought about rape. But it wasn't like what I'd heard about rape. I couldn't think about what happened with words. I just kept feeling it.
>
> My mother told me once that rape was when a man forced you to have sex with him. My cousin Lisa told me it was when a man pushed his thing in the private place between your legs and made you do it with him. She told me it was awful. I hadn't known exactly what my mother was talking about when she told me about rape. But I knew what Lisa meant.

If, through *Telling*, I sought to shine a light into the murky world of molestation, I couldn't shy away from specifics. There are only a few scenes as graphic as the preceding one in the book, but they are enough to let the reader know exactly what was happening.

Estelle and the Whispering Angel

I mentioned earlier that it was seeing the response my reluctant readers had to the unpublished *Telling* manuscript that kept me sending it out beyond the first ten rejections. But there was more to it than that. There was one girl in particular who changed the fate of the manuscript, and the ultimate direction of my life.

According to her file, Estelle read on a high second-grade level. Her writing was laborious. English was not her first language, and she had never in her life read a book in any language. But day after day, upon entering class, she got the *Telling* manuscript and read intently, four or five pages each period, her lips moving in silent formation of the words.

When Estelle finally finished the book, she was able to speak for the first time of something that had happened to her several years before, and to begin the process of healing deep wounds. This because of *Telling!*

Estelle's response convinced me to send the manuscript out to every publisher in the world, if need be, to ensure that other Estelles might also be emboldened by the story. Through *Telling*, Estelle heard the voice of the angel whispering "grow, grow." Through Estelle, I too heard the voice of the whispering angel.

If *Telling* had been weakened by avoiding all "bad" words, it probably would not have rung so true to Estelle, and to many readers who have come after her.

TELLING Offers Insight to Others

From a reader in Minnesota:

> I know that if I would have seen this book when I was eleven, when the same thing was happening to me, I might have had the courage to tell someone before it went too far. Your book gives a helping hand to all the hurting girls out there. . . .

From a reader in San Diego:

> *Telling* helped me to understand some things I was going through. I learned how to not keep something inside of me. . . .

Telling *Helps Low-Level Readers Become Eager Readers*

Teaching *Telling* to my ninth-grade "C" level classes has been the most successful and gratifying experience I have ever had. Usually, several of my students "forget" to bring their books to class, "forget" to do homework and even "forget" to come to class. However, from the first day we began reading *Telling,* I cannot recall a single student who was once without a book and the number of homework assignments which were completed increased dramatically.

Carol Schneider, Gabrieleno High School

As with *Telling*, when I started writing *Detour for Emmy*, I knew I didn't want a watered-down version of Emmy's experiences. Sexuality is too important an aspect of teen life to gloss over as if it barely exists. The novel takes Emmy through her first sexual awakening and the struggle of going through pregnancy and childbirth with no support, either from the baby's father or from Emmy's mother. It is a sad though, I hope, ultimately illuminating story.

Although *Detour for Emmy* is not riddled with graphic sex, there are a few scenes that occasionally get a reaction from self-appointed keepers of teen morality. Emmy *does* get pregnant, and it's not because of impurities in the water she drinks. Although she and her boyfriend practice safe sex, when they are at the beach one night he convinces her that the "pull-out" method is a good means of birth control. Later, when it is *too* late, the school nurse enlightens Emmy: "The old pull-out method. The world is full of cute little pullout babies. I could name seven from this school alone, just last year. Of course, I wouldn't betray any confidences . . . but they're all over the place."

Realistic Fiction Offers New Insights

If I had written around the issues, I doubt that I would have heard:

> That book made me realize where my life was going, which was somewhere I didn't want it to go.

> I'm a sixteen-year-old girl and I have a three-month-old baby boy. I quit school in January when I found out I was pregnant. When my son was born I had no intentions of going back to school or going to work. Mainly I depended on others to help, like the family I live with. I look up to Emmy. She's my idol, and now since I read this book I'm going back to full-time school and I'm going to find a part-time job.

> The struggles Emmy had to deal with made me sure I would not want to be in her position. I have decided to abstain from sex until marriage.

> Thank you for helping me see that I could make a life for myself and my baby.

. . . and so on.

Keeping the Language Real

Too Soon for Jeff, Beyond Dreams, But What About Me, Baby Help, If You Loved Me, and *Love Rules* all have sections that may be offensive to some. One of the last things I do before sending a manuscript off to the publisher is a "bad" word check. Can I substitute a gentler word for the potentially offensive one? Can I simply delete an expletive and still have a powerful and realistic piece of dialog? Most often not. In *Baby Help*, when Rudy, in a drunken rage, is beating up on Melissa, he's not likely to be saying, "Golly darn, you irritate me."

What a disservice I would have done to all of the Melissas out there, the ones who have vulgar profanity shouted at them day after day after day. To deny such reality would be to deny the truth of their horrendous experiences, to add to their sense of aloneness. I don't have the stomach for it.

Fear Breeds Ignorance

I was recently browsing through *American Libraries*, a magazine put out by the American Library Association. In the "Censorship Watch" column under the heading "Naughty Bits Perturb Indiana Parents," a parent says of *Detour for Emmy:* "I don't want my children reading that type of trash . . ." After several years of occasional challenges, it still shocks me to realize that I'm being portrayed as an evil influence on innocent youth, or to hear my books described as pornography. But I will not pander to would-be censors at the expense of realism.

Nancy Garden, author of many wonderful young adult novels, and no stranger to book challenges, writes:

> The fear that breeds censorship is usually fear of the unknown, fear that stems from misinformation, fear that books and movies almost automatically make people do bad things, fear that knowledge of more than a single set of ideas and standards will doom children to a horrible fate or will make them into monsters. It is a very real fear, and a mistake to dismiss it out of hand as inauthentic.

But the terrible thing about censorship is that when it is successful, it fosters more ignorance and, therefore, more fear. Each attempt at banning a book chips away at the First Amendment, a cornerstone of our democracy, and each attempt brings us a little closer to becoming a nation of sheep, blindly, unthinkingly following a single leader's vision.

Who Has the Right to Deny Materials for ALL Children?

In the case of the Indiana parent who didn't want her children reading trash, she and a few of her cohorts managed to get *Detour for Emmy* and *Life on the Color Line* removed from the shelves of the Rosedale Elementary School. I don't know about *Life on the Color Line*, but I can agree that *Detour for Emmy* is probably not appropriate for *most* elementary school students. What about the few for whom it is appropriate though? What about the high school sophomore who stood shyly outside a group of talkative students waiting for a quiet time? I was at their school for an author visit, and the talkative ones had plenty of questions. When they finally went on to other things, the shy girl handed me a well-worn copy of *Detour for Emmy*, asking if I would sign it to her—Sonya.

"This book changed my life," she said.

"Really? How?"

"I found it in the sixth grade, and I read it over and over."

"And how did that change things for you?"

"It taught me to be careful with my life—not to get all messed up, like my older sister did."

Sonya's a bright girl and is determined to do well in spite of some difficult circumstances. If it hadn't been *Detour for Emmy*, it would probably have been some other book. But I'm glad the protectors of innocent children were not ferreting out books in Sonya's library, or classroom, denying her and others like her access to meaningful materials.

Heroes in Our Midst

The real heroes in the censorship battle are educators who stand up to challenges in a way that brings reason to the process. One such educator is the principal of a middle school in a small town in Tennessee. *Detour for Emmy* was being challenged by a few fearful parents who wanted to restrict the reading choices of a whole school district. The principal wrote to me of the outcome of that situation:

> The Giles County School Board voted 4–3 to keep the book in the library. There were several letters to the editor where townspeople disagreed with their decision, but it has died down now.
>
> I stood my ground and didn't budge. It became a First Amendment right to be allowed to read the book, in my opinion. I persuaded the four members that it was not in the best interest of our county that we start censoring books in our libraries.
>
> When I went before the school board, I carried with me the definition, as given by the Supreme Court, as to what was pornography, since that's the accusation the woman made about the book. I went prepared with documents, definitions and a strong will.

Underhanded Censorship

As insidious as the public attacks on books can be, they are nothing compared to the murky, ill-defined, very effective practices of sub-rosa censorship. According to Harry Mazer (Blume 2001, 98), a highly respected and prolific writer of books for young readers:

> The negative effects of censorship don't always come out in the open. Where have my books been quietly removed from school shelves without any voices raised in protest? Where has a librarian or teacher chosen not to order my books rather than

risk arousing the censor? . . . We need more books. More authors. More varied points of view. Books are our windows on the world. They permit us to safely experience other lives and ways of thinking and feeling. Books give us a glimmer of the complexity and wonder of life. All this, the censor would deny us.

The following passage from *Love Rules* is fiction, but it follows closely a true experience that was passed on to me by a librarian at a conference where we were both attending a session on the topic of providing gay/lesbian students with materials that reflected something of their own lives. The librarian told of putting small rainbow stickers on the spine of books that offered such reflections. Here is the barely fictionalized account. Lynne, the best friend of Kit, a newly out-of-the-closet lesbian, is the narrator:

> When we went back to school after Winter Break, it seemed that the whole anti-gay thing had faded. No one was plastering insulting stickers all over, or making crude remarks to Frankie or Kit. . . . Not that everything was perfect. Emmy [the grown-up *Detour* character and now the librarian at Hamilton High School] noticed that several books with rainbow stickers on them were missing from the shelves. How could they get past the library's new and supposedly foolproof security system? When she did a computer search, she found that fifteen of those titles had been checked out during one week's time. Most had gone to members of the Christ First group. Two had been checked out by Eric's younger sister. There was nothing wrong with that, except we all doubted those particular students were trying to educate themselves regarding lesbian, gay, bi, and trans issues.
>
> It wasn't until March that Emmy realized that all of the rainbow stickered books were missing from the shelves. They were all legally checked out, but not one had been returned. When Emmy called homes about the books, she would always be answered politely and get a promise that the book would be returned the next day, but they never were.
>
> Nicole wrote an editorial for the school newspaper, saying such tactics were dishonest—the sneakiest form of censorship. We took turns writing letters to the editor of the *Hamilton Heights Daily News*, so there would be at least one a week. We pointed to the hypocrisy of so-called Christians who stole school property. We questioned where theft fit into the ideals of "Americans for Family Values."

The Toll on Imagination

The emotional toll that censorship takes on writers must also be reckoned with. Again, from Harry Mazer:

> I struggle each day not to let the fear of the censor poison my writing. Where the censor rules, a dull sameness creeps into books. Am I becoming cautious, being too

careful in what I choose to write about, watching my language? It's this caution inside that I fear, more than the censors. If I can't write the book that I want to write, what am I doing?

And from Julius Lester (Blume 2001, 52):

> There are times when I write something and am afraid that this one might "get me in trouble" again. But what is the alternative? To write and not tell the truth? That would be death for any writer. But more, it would be death to the imagination. And if the imagination dies, what will happen to the souls of children?

Fighting Censorship

How *do* we combat the forces that would silence diverse voices? How *do* we oppose censorship? (TOTT, pp. 101–103) One of the main lines of defense for schools and libraries is to have a well thought out challenge policy in place, and to familiarize faculty with the policy.

It helps to back up potentially controversial books with positive reviews, lists of awards, and inclusions in "best books" lists. School librarians are generally very helpful in gathering such information and also very knowledgeable about the how-tos of meeting challenges.

There are many national organizations that offer information and help regarding issues of censorship. The important thing is not to fold at the first sign of controversy, but to work through the issues at stake in a reasonable, previously determined manner.

Birth of an Intellectual Freedom Warrior

Judy Blume tells of an experience with *Tiger Eyes*, when she was pressured to remove lines alluding to masturbation, pressured to go against her strongest instincts about the importance of those lines.

Judy Blume is one of those rare writers who can be thigh-slappingly funny in one paragraph and have you in tears in the next. *Tiger Eyes* is a wonderful story and when I read it many years ago, I did not sense that there was anything missing that should have been there. Maybe the story is better without the expurgated lines. Who can say? Ultimately, that's not the point. The point is that an excellent writer had been discouraged and demoralized by going against what *she* knew to be true to the story.

The only good news to be gleaned from the *Tiger Eyes* story is that it ultimately turned Ms. Blume into a strong and mighty voice for intellectual freedom, leading her to be a beacon to writers who sit alone, watching the squirrels, and wondering what they're doing with their lives.

Readers Ask

Dear Ms. R,

I teach in a very conservative community. Can you send me a list of interesting books that no one can object to?

Value My Job

Dear Value,

I understand your concern, but it is not realistic. Teachers don't get fired over a book choice, unless it's something you pick up at the local porno shop, or you absolutely refuse to follow district policy if you're asked to remove a particular book from your shelves, or you insist a student read something that her parent has demanded she not read. But you're not going to do those things.

What I hope you'll do is be brave in your selection of books, choosing them based on likely student interest. If you have as your criteria avoiding books that might possibly be objectionable, your selection field will be narrowed to zero. There is *no* book that is free from the possibility of objection by someone, somewhere.

M.R.

P.S. For names of organizations that support intellectual freedom, see TOTT: Be Prepared for Book Challenges.

Dear Ms. R,

The school district's bus drivers sometimes hold evening workshops in my classroom. Recently one of the drivers removed eight books from my shelves. She took them to the principal, with many supposedly objectionable sections underlined, and demanded that the books not ever be made available to students again. Among the books she had removed were Catcher in the Rye, Huckleberry Finn, *and* The Giver. *My principal stood behind me and the books are back on my shelves, but I feel [the woman] crossed a boundary that should have been respected and now I'm very nervous about the bus drivers using my room. What can I do?*

Tempted to Change the Locks

Dear Tempted,

Ask your principal to help you get the meetings moved to a different classroom. Also suggest that he file a report detailing the woman's vandalism of school property. Good luck.

M.R.

Questions Only You Can Answer

○ What would you do if one of your classroom books was challenged?

○ Do you self-censor, keeping "hit" books from your readers for the sake of avoiding possible controversy?

○ Think about a book you read as a teen that your parents might not have approved of had they known. Did that book harm you?

Chapter Five
Bibliotherapy Is Not a Four-Letter Word

*It matters, if individuals are to retain any capacity to form their own
judgments and opinions, that they continue to read for themselves. . . .
Why they read must be for and in their own interest.*
How to Read and Why, Harold Bloom

Reading versus Busywork

Irma stood waiting at the door, eager to continue the book she had started the
week before. According to her file, she read on a third-grade level. Her home language was Spanish, but she didn't read well in Spanish either. For the two months
that Irma had been in my fourth-period reading class, she fought my requirement
that everyone read from a book of his or her choice for twenty minutes each day.
A quiet, sullen loner, Irma saw no reason to waste her time by reading.

"I want to do *work*," she insisted. "I want to get credit."

"You get credit for reading."

"But I can get more credit doing worksheets."

"Not in this class you can't."

"I want to go back to Ms. V's class."

"Ms. V's class is filled," I always claimed.

Every day, while other students got their books and settled in to read, Irma and I had the same conversation. She begged for worksheets. I put tried-and-true favorites in front of her: *Deliver Us From Evie; Are You There God, It's Me Margaret; The Outsiders; Down These Mean Streets*—books that other struggling readers often connected with, stretching their skills for the sake of a compelling story.

I even gave Irma books that were officially designated "high-interest low-vocabulary." Although such books are consistently not as high-interest in reality as publishers claim, I was desperate enough to drag some from the dusty shelf behind the TV and offer them up.

Every day at the end of reading time I asked Irma if she wanted to keep any one of the books I had placed before her. The answer was always a sulky no, coupled with another plea for "real work."

Eureka!

Then, one happy Tuesday, after doing my stint with Irma and going back to my own reading, I glanced up from my book and saw that she had actually opened one of the books I'd put on her desk. At the end of reading time when I asked if she wanted to keep any of the books, she shoved *When She Hollers* by Cynthia Voight into her folder.

A week later, she was the first one settled at a table, reading before the bell rang.

"I can take my book home today," she told me, her tone confrontational, as if expecting an argument from me.

I checked her folder. "Right. Today's the day," I agreed.

One of my class requirements was that a student read a book in class for at least five days before checking it out. We lost fewer books that way. I'm not sure why, but my guess is that once a student loves a book he or she is much less likely to lose it.

Life Sucks

Irma finished *When She Hollers* within a few days after checking it out, then filled out the brief, but required, Book Completion Form (TOTT, pp. 104–105). In answer to the "What does this book say about life?" question, she wrote, "Life sucks."

After reading a book, the last phase before credit gets signed off on contract cards is a short conference with the teacher. Irma told me a bit about the book. I let her get by with a very little bit because I knew she had read the book, and I knew she didn't like to talk, especially not to teachers, maybe even especially not to me. I mentioned her "life sucks" interpretation of the theme of the book, and agreed with her that life does sometimes suck. But I claimed that it also sometimes soars. We talked about the main character, Tish, in *When She Hollers*, and how she fought her stepfather and overcame his brutality.

"She'll never forget her asshole stepdad," Irma said. "She'll never forget what he did."

"Right. She's been hurt, and she'll always carry the scars. But do you think things can get better for her?"

"What do *you* think," she asked, the confrontational tone back, full scale.

"I don't know. I suppose it could go either way. But she's been strong, and brave, and maybe she's past the worst time of her life. I think there's at least a good chance that things can get better."

"But they don't always," Irma says.

"No. They don't. Sometimes life keeps on sucking."

Irma Kicks the "Work" Addiction

Irma renewed her quest for "work." I put another three books in front of her, two more by Cynthia Voight and Toni Morrison's *The Bluest Eye*, which deals with molestation and a host of other "life sucks" events. She chose *The Bluest Eye*.

By the end of the semester, Irma had read four novels that dealt with molestation. She hadn't asked for "work" in months.

A Defective Listening Gene

The school counselor and I were not soul mates. When I first started teaching at the M.H.S. alternative school, Mr. E would barge into my classroom and talk loudly about what a great teacher my predecessor had been. "It was amazing how he got these kids reading!" Mr. E would boom out, oblivious to the fact that my students had been engrossed in their own reading until he blew in. Having never taught, he was given to carrying on about the efficacy of various education theories and what we should be doing with "these" kids. At first I would try to have a conversation with him, but it soon became obvious that he'd emerged from the womb with a defective listening gene and that conversation with him was not an option.

In spite of his official "counselor" designation, students generally avoided Mr. E. "Man, that dude'll talk you to death and back!" one of our hippie throwbacks claimed.

Mr. E's Redeeming Quality and Futile Attempt at Time Management

Mr. E did, though, keep careful track of students' credits and progress toward graduation, and he helped several of them qualify for special job-training programs. I managed to respect what he offered and, like the students, avoided his monologues.

So . . . when Mr. E asked that I see him in his office after school, about Irma, I told him I needed to keep it short because of an appointment. My appointment was with the grocery store, but I was sure that even shopping was more important to me than whatever Mr. E might have to say, and say, and say.

When I entered his office with its constantly hissing air purifier and carefully tended bromeliads, Mr. E closed the door, then pulled his special Relax-the-Back chair around to sit closer to me. It seemed an unnatural and unnecessary gesture, probably a technique pounded into him in his counseling credentials courses. Why hadn't they pounded in listening skills instead?

He gave me a long look, sighed, and then expressed his very deep concern about the way in which I ran my classes.

Warned Against Bibliotherapy

"Bibliotherapy is a very sensitive process . . ." he began.

I completed my mental shopping list during Mr. E's lengthy monologue on the history and practice of bibliotherapy. The lecture ended with him telling me that I lacked the necessary training and credentials to be using "such methods" in my classroom, and that I was "out of bounds."

I was uncharacteristically speechless.

"Irma G. is in your reading class, is she not?"

If I hadn't already known that this was not a friendly meeting, the "is she not" would have been a certain tip-off.

"Irma's in my class, and doing very well. Why?"

"When I called her in for a credit check, she happened to let slip that you are practicing bibliotherapy in your reading classes . . ."

"Irma said 'bibliotherapy'?"

"No. But I know bibliotherapy when it's described to me! She told me that the books she's been reading in your classroom are helping her figure out some things about her life."

"Oh, my God! No!" I said, in mock dismay.

"This is no joke! Therapy in the hands of untrained practitioners can be very damaging! If counseling is to be done on this campus, it is to take place in this office, not in the classroom!"

"Can you please explain to me what it is I'm doing that falls under the category of bibliotherapy?"

"You're using books to analyze your students. You're assigning books that relate to their individual problems. I've been talking with other students as I do their credit checks and Irma is not the only one who thinks she's getting some personal help through reading assignments . . ."

Mr. E sputtered on past my supermarket appointment time. He gave various examples of the dangers of any kind of therapy in the hands of amateurs. He objected to the question on my Book Completion Form that asked what the book had to say about life. He questioned my competence as a reading teacher because I was assigning books to students that were too difficult for them. He knew their test scores and he saw students walking around with books that were obviously way beyond them. Why was I setting them up for failure? And on, and on, and on, as I gazed out the window at what would soon become the setting sun.

Trial-and-Error Book Selections

If Mr. E had been blessed with an intact listening gene, I would have told him that I didn't "assign" books, that the books were selected by students through a process of trial and error, and that their test scores obviously didn't reflect their true reading ability for material that was of interest to them. I would have admitted that once I found an author or subject with which a student seemed to connect, I kept offering books of the same ilk. I would also have admitted that their reading did sometimes encourage students to mention difficulties in their lives. "You know how the dad in that book was always drunk?" a student might ask.

I would nod.

"My dad's like that."

I would nod again. That was pretty much the extent of my bibliotherapeutic practices, although at least one of the next three books I put before that particular reader would include a character who drank too much.

A Hunger for Books That Reflect Life

A number of students love Harry Potter, the C. S. Lewis Narnia series, science fiction, and Stephen King, but the majority of at-risk students are hungry to read something that reflects life as they know it. Hungry to find something that allows them to think they're not the only ones with big problems and that allows them to consider such problems at a safe distance. Through reading, Irma could be carried into Tish's world and experience the complexities of that character's response to a horrible situation. It was much easier for Irma to think about Tish's asshole stepfather than it was to think about her own. Maybe reading about people with whom we sense a commonality *is* bibliotherapy, but I wasn't the practitioner. My students were. Irma was her own therapist as she gravitated toward stories that reached her soul and shed a beam of light into dark places.

The Healing Power of Books

I might also have reminded Mr. E—had I been able to gain his figurative ear, of certain statistics—that of the people who receive professional therapy, about one-third get better, one-third get worse, and one-third stay the same.

Many of us, particularly those in the at-risk category, do not seek, or cannot afford, professional help. We muddle through on our own, trying to heal the scars and fill in the empty spaces. Friends help us do this. Love helps us do this. Books help us do this.

I might have told Mr. E that I would continue trying to find books that would worm their way into the souls and psyches of my students. But I didn't. When I left his office, I was no longer in the mood either for grocery shopping or cooking. I decided to take my husband and son out to dinner. That gave me enough time to swing by the bookstore for a quick browse. In the Young Adult section I found a book by Chris Crutcher that dealt with a father's brutality. I bought it to have on hand when Irma finished her present book. I'd place that on her desk, along with another book by Toni Morrison and a new Cynthia Voight.

The Importance of Free Choice

Is it a mistake not to demand that the Irmas in our classrooms expand their reading choices beyond "life sucks" stories?

Whenever I ask myself that question, I remember that there was a time in my life when I read nothing but Nancy Drew mysteries. In high school I was on a Mickey Spillane kick. Here's what I didn't read during my coming-of-age years: *Silas Marner,* "Julius Caesar," *The Scarlet Letter, Great Expectations,* "Macbeth."

I'm not sure why I hungered for Nancy Drew, or Mickey Spillane. I can guess that I needed to think it was possible for a girl to take charge, to be the only one who could figure out how to overcome evil and make things right. As for Mickey Spillane? Maybe it was rebellion. They were simply the dirtiest books I could get my hands on at the time.

Reading for Life

Whatever my reasons, I enjoyed what I read. I'm still reading, though I'm not still reading Nancy Drew or Mickey Spillane. I have, in fact, somewhere along the way, read and enjoyed all of the books that were assigned in my junior high and high school classes. But I read them when they had something to say to me, when my soul was big enough that I could cry for Pip rather than being bored by him.

And Irma? Long after she graduated she would occasionally drop by and ask for reading suggestions. She never asked for work. "Work" is a game played to pile up credits. Reading is for life.

READERS ASK

Dear Ms. R,

Did you report Irma's case to the authorities? It sounds as if she'd been abused by her father. Reporting such a suspicion is mandated in my state, isn't it in yours?

Ms. Curious

Dear Curious,

Yes, as educators we are mandated to report knowledge or even suspicion of abuse, neglect, a plan to harm one's self or others, or behavior that is life threatening (TOTT, pp. 107–108). If I'd had any confidence in Mr. E's ability to handle sensitive issues, I would have reported the case to him. Instead, I made an informal report to the nurse, whom I trusted. It turned out that Irma's father was in prison and was no longer a threat to her. She and her mother were already in counseling. The nurse made the necessary phone call to social services, who took the report but did not see a need to take action under Irma's present circumstances.

M.R.

Dear Ms. R,

You keep talking about finding the "hit" book. What about magazines and newspapers?

Why Not?

Dear W.N.,

I've forever straddled the fence on this one. On the plus side, magazines and newspapers sometimes engage students who are intimidated by books, or who want to know the latest Hollywood gossip about a teen idol or sports hero. The problem is that some students will only flip through such publications, glancing at the pictures but not settling on anything to read. Janice Pilgreen, in *The SSR Handbook*, tells of a system she uses in her classrooms. Students may have one period of browsing through a magazine's pictures and articles. By the end of the period, they choose an article of interest to read for the following day. This makes sense. Somewhere along the way I would hope to see the magazine reader get connected with a book, but that may be more about my own personal compulsions than it is about establishing a "reading for life" habit.

M.R.

Questions Only You Can Answer

❍ Do I sometimes give in to "busywork" during SSR rather than insist for the thousandth time that the most stubborn non-reader must read?

❍ If I am uncomfortable with the repetitious choice of a certain topic, such as drugs, mayhem, religion, do I pressure the student into reading something more to *my* liking?

❍ What's the difference between pressure and guidance?

Chapter Six
What Makes for a Successful SSR Program?

The words of the book cover her as comfortably as a blanket on a cold night. She can wrap herself in the warmth of them. She can rest here. The noise of the shovels and axes is replaced with the sweet drop of words falling from her mind into the empty chamber of her heart.

Afterimage, Helen Humphreys

An SSR Program for Juvenile Offenders

I recently had the great good fortune to help set up a Sustained Silent Reading program at Esperanza Junior/Senior High School, which is run by the Sacramento County Office of Education at the Warren E. Thornton Youth Center in Sacramento. It is a residential school—a dual agency cooperative—and offers juvenile offenders an interlude between release from juvenile hall and return home, or placement in a group home, or other foster care setting. It is a coed facility, though there are generally more boys than girls in their constantly changing enrollment.

The Esperanza student body consists of fifty students, give or take one or two on any given day. They are there for seven weeks, preparing to continue their education on "the outs." The school offers academic classes in social studies, English, math, and science, plus an elective. In addition to the basic classroom work, some prepare for the G.E.D., while others work on the specific skills needed to pass the state's high school exit exam. There also are counseling programs run by outside agencies that offer help with a variety of problems, including substance abuse and anger management.

Preparations

After conversations with the school's principal and teacher-in-charge, I met with the Esperanza staff, including the clerical staff, classroom aides, and on-campus probation officers. We talked about the importance of reading for pleasure and discussed Simple Ways to Encourage a Reading Habit (TOTT, p. 113).

There was strong support from the administration and the staff was generally enthused. The few who weren't so enthused were not actively fighting the program—an important factor in any all-school SSR program.

What's in a Name?

We decided we needed a catchier phrase than Sustained Silent Reading, or SSR, to identify the new program, so I emailed teachers with a few of the hundreds of possible acronyms I'd come across somewhere along the way:

DEAR—Drop Everything and Read
RIOT—Reading Is Our Thing
RIP—Read in Peace
SAFARI—Students and Faculty All Read Independently
SUPER—Silent Undisturbed Private Entertainment Reading
SURE—Sustained Uninterrupted Reading Enjoyment

RIP and RIOT were immediately thrown out because of the myriad connotations both words held for Esperanza students. SAFARI was the acronym of choice, and the staff made good use of the "safari" theme (TOTT, p. 114).

In preparing for any SAFARI, supplies and provisions must be brought on board. At Esperanza, a SAFARI folder, complete with Reading Logs and the SAFARI flyer, was ready for each student on day one of the new program. More than a hundred new books were on hand, obtained with the help of probation department funds. These books included many of the titles recommended on the Mirrors of the Soul—Windows to Others book list (TOTT, pp. 115–120).

The Kickoff

On "kickoff" day, I entered the lobby of the youth center and saw that creative staff members had covered the bulletin board in a striking jungle print, which was the background for a colorful display of book jackets and author information. Many staff members were wearing jungle print shirts, which added a festive touch.

Students filed into the common meeting room at eight in the morning of the first day. All wore white tee shirts and khaki pants. They entered in an orderly manner, single file, according to their class assignments. Probation officers and/or teachers were quick to confront the slightest unruliness. It is a requirement that students, when walking from one place to another, keep their thumbs in the waistband of their pants—the epitome of the "keep your hands to yourself" rule.

I talked with the group about the importance of reading, not only for success in school and in later life, but for the sake of their own emotional and spiritual development. Of course, none of that talk is worth a hill of beans until they've had the experience of connecting with a book on a deep level. But I can't help myself. I have to say it anyway.

We also talked about how each person has his/her own unique stories to tell, and no one can tell those stories the way he/she can. I used slides to show where some of my ideas have come from, and also to show various sources of research. I read a few pages from "Only If You Think So," which is a short story in my *Beyond Dreams* book. It tells of a boy on a downhill slide, recently kicked out of the local comprehensive high school and sent to an alternative school. Low-achieving students generally appreciate this story, and the Esperanza group was no exception.

For Most, Reading Is Boring

In a show of hands, only four students said they liked to read, and that they read for pleasure. The questionnaires they all filled out at the end of our assembly showed that a vast majority of students thought reading was "boring," and a "waste of time," although many of them said they read the newspaper. A few mentioned a book they might like to read and several expressed interest in reading one of the books I had mentioned in my introductory remarks.

Teacher Support

Teachers welcomed me into their classrooms, even though my interruptions probably didn't fit with their lesson plans. Because of their openness, I was able to do booktalks in the math classroom, and read aloud in the social studies classroom. I could also talk quietly with individual students who had expressed their lack of enthusiasm for the SAFARI program in their questionnaire comments, and to help them find a book that might possibly be of interest to them.

A Community of Readers

Like most teachers, Esperanza teachers have not had the time to develop a vast awareness of Young Adult books. But I have, and I delight in spreading that awareness around (TOTT, pp. 115–120). By the beginning of the first SAFARI class, several of the most reluctant readers (according to their questionnaires) had expressed a willingness to at least try a book I'd recommended.

The basic SAFARI plan was for students and staff to read from a book of their choice for twenty-five minutes, every day, during fourth period. Some students were guided to, or found, "hit" books immediately. Others took longer to connect with a book. By the end of the second week though, most students were reading something of interest to them, and they looked forward to SAFARI time. So did teachers. Almost overnight, it seemed, there was casual talk about books—students and teachers talking about the books they were reading, and expressing an interest in what others were reading. They were becoming a community of readers.

A Thrilling Experience

One of my biggest thrills as a writer/teacher occurred at Esperanza. On the first day, after the kickoff assembly, Tony, who was very tough looking, waited to talk with me. Head down, not making eye contact, he said, "Can I read that book *Telling?*"

"Sure," I said. "I'll have it waiting for you in your SAFARI classroom."

He looked up at me, revealing extremely dark, brown, sad-looking eyes. "About the girl who gets molested?" he asked.

"That's the one."

Later, when I stopped by Tony's classroom with *my* book of choice and sat quietly reading with the class, I noticed that Tony seemed absorbed in *Telling*. At the end of the reading period he caught my attention and said quietly, "This is a good book, even if I don't like to read."

A couple of weeks later he proudly showed me that he only had one more chapter to go. "I'll finish it tomorrow," he said. "This is the first book I've ever read, and it's really good."

The boy sitting across from Tony said he also thought *Telling* was a really good book.

"Are you reading *Telling* too?" I asked.

"He's reading it to me at night," he said, gesturing toward Tony.

They were roommates, and Tony was reading to him every night before lights out. These were two boys who had never before had any interest in reading or books. Not only that, but they were reading a very sensitive story about a twelve-year-old girl—not exactly a topic one would expect hard-core lawbreakers to choose.

When Tony finished the book, he told me that he thought it had helped him understand what his sister had been through.

The Students Say "Thanks"

After four weeks of daily SSR, I asked students to complete evaluation forms, and to write on the back any comments they would like to make about their SAFARI experiences. I was amazed with the number of notes that either started or ended with "thank you." Or sometimes both:

> "Thank you for this reading program you have given me. Now I am more into books than I used to be. Right now I am reading a book called *The Wicked Heart*. It is the best book I have ever read. Thank you."

> "By reading your books shows me that I got more reading skills than I thought I had. Thank you."

> "I didn't read anything on the outs, and now I read all the time. Thank you."

> Was it 100 percent? Well . . . no.

> "I can only read easy books. I think that in 4th period it is boring because we read too long."

Students Evaluate SSR

In response to the evaluation statement, "As a result of SAFARI, I expect to continue reading regularly and independently even when I am no longer at Esperanza," four students answered "No way."

On the other hand, 81 percent said that they would either definitely or probably continue reading regularly even after they leave Esperanza. In addition, 67 percent of SAFARI participants thought their reading skills improved either a little or a lot, and 79 percent said their interest in reading had improved either a little or a lot.

I asked them to rate several aspects of SAFARI on a scale of 1 to 10. The overall program rating was 8.6, even with the three students who rated everything a zero. (I included them in the calculations, but changed the zeroes to ones, since zero had not been an option on the form.)

The ratings were: "free choice of books," 9.6; "reading on my own twenty-five minutes a day," 8.5; "the right to change books whenever I want," 9.0. Their lowest rating was for "writing in my Reading Log," 7.2. But even 7.2 is an impressive rating for students who, except for two or three, had been extremely unmotivated, low achievers most of their academic lives.

Results That Cannot Be Measured

One of the unpredictable and hard-to-measure factors in any SSR program has to do with whether it *really* builds a lifelong reading habit, or only increases the time students spend reading for pleasure while they are in the program. It's impossible to generalize, but I was pleased with a conversation I had with Roberto, who had been released just before my official SAFARI time was up.

When I dropped in for a visit not long ago, Roberto was back. Although the standard time spent at Esperanza is seven weeks, if an ex-student commits a new offense or violates probation, the court may recommit him or her.

"Tell me," I said to the recently returned Roberto, "when you were wherever you were when you weren't here, were you still reading?"

He laughed his most delightful laugh. "Sure, I read all the time now. You guys made me *have* to read."

The Press Acknowledges Kids' Potential—Worthy of Respect

A few months into the program, the *Sacramento Bee* sent one of their top columnists, Anita Creamer, to Esperanza to report on the SAFARI program. She interviewed students, school staff, and probation staff, and, after jumping through hoops to get permission from a judge, a *Bee* photographer took pictures. The pictures could not show the faces of any wards of the court, so *Bee* readers saw backs of students reading at their desks with a teacher facing them. Even so, it turned out to be a very upbeat and compelling article. Positive publicity was nothing Esperanza students often, if ever, experienced. This was made obvious to me on my very first visit to Esperanza.

Usually, if some sweet misguided student refers to my "fame," I confess that I am far from famous. But when an Esperanza student told me she couldn't believe that a famous author would ever come to a school like theirs, I let the illusion stay put.

When students saw and read the *Bee* spread, they were absolutely thrilled. Ms. Creamer quoted the Chief Deputy of the Sacramento County Probation Department, saying "The program is really valuable to the commitment facility . . ." It "shows that if we take the time to guide children in the right direction, they're receptive to change. When kids are reading in their rooms at night, you know it's a success."

Obviously a word person, Ms. Creamer wrote:

What an astonishing gift—to learn to finish a book; to grasp for the first time that reading, far from a tedious classroom chore, is relevant to your existence. And to begin to understand that life without the joys and benefits of the written word is a stunningly barren, narrow path.

The article went on to point out that not all of Sacramento's kids have had books read to them, or even available to them. Not all have had parental guidance on their paths through school:

Imagine the homes with no books at all, no written material except the bills that come with the daily mail. Reading is far from valued. Education is, at best, someone else's opportunity—at worst, a way to fail.

For many of Esperanza's students, SAFARI is a new start.

What a treat that was for those who are often thought of as lost, or as drains on society, to be written about with respect for their achievements and possibilities. And what an important message that is to the greater community—these kids are worthy, with plenty of potential, given half a chance.

Continued Success for SSR at Esperanza

Esperanza's continued success is due to the enthusiasm and teamwork of the whole staff, and to *their* continued interest in their own personal reading. Without their enthusiasm, there would be no follow-up on the TOTT: Simple Ways to Encourage a Reading Habit. Books would not be exchanged and recommended among students *and* staff. SAFARI would be a lip-service-only experiment, and it wouldn't work. But it *does* work, beautifully. One of the teachers stated: "It is of course the fact that *we* are reading along with the students, that the real modeling for pleasure reading takes place. It is not an issue of do as I say, not as I do . . . quite the contrary!"

Another factor in the SAFARI success has to do with the rigid discipline to which these wards of the court must conform—a factor totally beyond the control of most classroom teachers. At Esperanza, students don't show up for class in the morning, hungry, hungover, under the influence of a controlled substance, or having simply been up all night. They've had lights out at 10:00 and breakfast at 7:30 in the morning. Except for rare cases of verified illness, no one is absent. The downside of this is, of course, that these are very troubled kids, usually with good reason; and, in spite of the strong discipline, there are plenty of roadblocks to their academic achievement. But they've learned to connect with books that may, we can only hope, be a much-needed saving grace.

Perfection Is Not a Requirement

It is heartening to see youth offenders excited by books and reading, but such responses to SSR are by no means rare. From California to New York to Florida, I've visited schools where dedicated teachers, librarians, and administrators are bringing the joy of reading to both struggling and advanced readers. These programs vary according to the personalities of the schools and their personnel. All are highly effective. All have minor problems. Luckily, perfection is not a requirement for an effective SSR program.

Not All SSR Programs Are Effective

Although no two successful SSR programs are exactly alike, they do incorporate many of the same practices. As much as I like talking about the successes though, I would be remiss if I neglected to mention practices that can drag SSR into the pit of mediocrity. Simple Ways to *Discourage* a Reading Habit (TOTT, pp. 121–122) offers a thorough look at negative practices, but I would like to emphasize a few here, before you get to the Tricks of the Trade section.

Many of the things that discourage SSR are apparent: not having a variety of books, not respecting the student's choice of reading materials, not having readily accessible books, not providing a good reading model or environment.

Roadblocks to Lifelong Reading Habits

Other discouraging practices are a bit more vague. Certain schedules can be discouraging. If you can only have SSR for fifteen minutes on Monday and Friday, it's better than nothing, but it's really not enough. If you must limit SSR to two days, at least have them be consecutive, preferably midweek—Tuesday and Wednesday or Wednesday and Thursday. It is hard enough for reluctant readers to latch on to a book without having several days between reading blocks.

Reluctant readers are easily discouraged, and they are also often less than totally responsible in a school setting. However, it's not supportive of SSR goals to focus on the student's irresponsibility on occasions of forgotten books, lost folders, and/or incomplete Reading Log records. And although we must do the best we can to keep books from getting lost, if we have rules that a student can't check a new book out until she returns the previous one, we're not encouraging a reading habit. A constant question to ourselves should be "Is what I'm about to say or do encouraging this student, or will it be discouraging?"

Some students will have a favorite book that they want to read over and over again. It is discouraging not to allow them to do so. In truth, we never read the same book twice, because each time *we* bring something new to it. They're continuing to read it for reasons we don't understand, but it's important to respect their choice.

Another roadblock to a successful SSR program can be the negative attitudes of even a few staff members. The most effective way to deal with this is to combine energies with those who *are* supportive of SSR. You cannot make anyone else's SSR program work, but you can continue to strengthen your own by moving forward in spite of the naysayers. Sometimes, miracle of miracles, when teachers who were resistant to SSR in the beginning see it at work, they become more open to trying the program.

Basic Training

Along these same lines, it is important that teachers have some basic SSR training before starting a new program. It sounds very simple—everyone including the teacher reads silently for twenty minutes a day. Why have yet another series of workshops for that? Well, in reality, because SSR demands more than the obvious.

READERS ASK

Dear Ms. R,

It seems to me that one of the main reasons the SAFARI program was so successful was because of the captive audience. What about the rest of us, whose students are out all night and think of SSR as a chance to catch a few winks?

Sick of Snoozers

Dear S.O.S.,

Right. The Esparanza students were not out carousing, ingesting drugs or alcohol—three hots and a cot is more than many students on "the outs" get. At the risk of sounding like a broken record, a "hit" book will make all the difference. I'll admit it may not have the carouser reading to his friends at night, but it will do wonders for him during SSR.

For the sake of your sanity, the snoozer's safety, and the SSR program—no snoozing in class. He/she may have had a big dose of the drug-of-the-month before coming to your class. You definitely don't want the short snooze to turn into the endless sleep on your watch. Refer the sleeper to the nurse, if you're lucky enough to have one on your campus. If not, ask for an evaluation from whoever watches over such things on a district level. Act as if it's a medical problem rather than a running wild problem. It may be. Or it may be long hours at a fast-food job, which we know is illegal, but not unusual. Unless it's a true medical problem, your snoozers won't like the referrals, which may be enough to cure their insomnia, at least in *your* classroom.

M.R.

Dear Ms. R,

I'm envious of a school-wide program that has everyone reading at the same time every day. Where I teach, most of the staff thinks it's a waste to take time away from their usual curriculum and let students "just sit and read." How can I make them understand the value of SSR?

Mr. Minority Opinion

Dear Mr. M,

You can talk until you're blue in the face and still not change any closed, hardened minds. My advice to you is the same advice you probably give your writing students: "Show, don't tell."

M.R.

Questions Only You Can Answer

○ Am I worried about what other teachers or administrators think if they come into my classroom and see that we are all reading silently?

○ Do they think I'm being lazy or do they think, "Wow! All of these kids are on-task, reading, and she's being a great role model"?

○ Do I assign complicated book reports, writing assignments that ask for analyses of literary devices, or other activities that have the reluctant reader dreading to finish his/her book?

○ Do I keep in mind that we're working toward establishing habits that translate to real-life reading?

Chapter Seven

Why Bother with the Ones Who Can't or Won't Get with the Program?

School explains only so much about a student. The largest
clues to success or failure lie beyond Seward Park's
[school's] portals, in the home and on the street.
Small Victories, Samuel Freedman

I Can't Read and You Can't Teach Me—the Dilemma of Herman

Herman was one of those who *couldn't* get with the program. A Big Baby Huey kind of guy, he had a mouth that even his peers were soon sick of. Although he was seventeen, he had failed so many classes that he was still officially categorized as a ninth grader. He'd been in my reading class for several weeks, said he couldn't read, and he wouldn't try.

When he came to class reeking of marijuana, I suspended him for three days. He decried the injustice of it all. Herman claimed he'd only done it for me. I wanted him to work on reading, and he could do better with a buzz. Now, I'd gone and suspended him for trying to do better! He could do a lot of things better after several tokes, like drive a car, take care of his little brother, play basketball, concentrate, and get along with his mom.

A Simple Evaluation

Except for the few obvious excellent readers, my practice was to do an informal WRAT (Wide Range Achievement Test) with students to keep in their folders, along with their Reading Questionnaires and Reading Log sheets. The reading segment of a WRAT takes five to ten minutes to administer and provides a fairly accurate "guestimate" of most students' reading levels. It doesn't reveal that a student, like Herman, can recognize and say words but not comprehend text; however, that glitch is quickly revealed in other ways.

Herman's test placed him somewhere in the mid-fifth-grade range. It soon became obvious that although he could say the words, he couldn't comprehend the meaning of a paragraph that contained the words. He had a thorough understanding of the stories I read aloud to the class. He had a strong narrative sense that, to my great consternation, he exhibited orally and forcefully during SSR.

A Master of Distraction

When Herman returned to class after his suspension, he was still angry. He complained loudly about his unjust treatment. He proclaimed that reading was useless and those who spent their time that way were fools. Herman was, to offer the epitome of understatement, disruptive.

I walked him out of class and admitted that I couldn't make him read, but I wouldn't tolerate behavior that distracted others from their reading. That worked for a few minutes.

What to Do with Herman?

I called his mother to enlist her help. This is a mother who had been getting calls from Herman's teachers for the past eleven years. My guess, while talking with her, was that *her* mother had received calls about *her* all through school.

I brought his name up during a faculty meeting. His other teachers were equally frustrated with Herman. The one thing at which he was successful was cleaning out the rabbit cages for the petting zoo. I couldn't figure out how to transfer that strength to the reading classroom.

Unfortunately for him, but fortunate for the peace and sanctity of our class, Herman was absent more often than he was in attendance. When he did come to school, I read with him from *Midnight Express*, which had been made into a movie of the same name and was one of his favorite movies. As with several other students, I read a sentence, then he read a sentence, then we talked about the meaning. He did all right with that, but he couldn't get the meaning of the next paragraph when he read it on his own.

Herman's History

In the service of keeping an open mind, it was my practice not to look at a student's records until I'd known him or her for a while. After three or four weeks, I took a look at Herman's file. I would have predicted that he was sent to us for drug use or chronic truancy. Wrong. He was sent our way for having thrown a chair at a teacher.

Herman had been in all manner of special programs from first grade on. He had been given numerous evaluations, both psychological and academic, and referrals to a variety of doctors and institutions for more diagnostic procedures. It was not obvious from his file whether there had been consistent follow-through on referrals or not. It *was* obvious that his teachers had been greatly frustrated while working with him. Some had seen his sweet side and struggled mightily to help him adapt and advance. Others saw him as hopeless and wanted him placed anywhere but in *their* classrooms. Where to go with a student for whom all known resources had failed?

My goal with Herman became simply to keep him from disrupting the other readers. That put me in the same class as the currently much-maligned "teachers with low expectations." At the time my decision seemed in line with a slight variation of the ubiquitous serenity prayer. I accepted what I could not change—Herman's ongoing reading problems—and gathered the courage to change that which I might—Herman's disruptive behavior.

Herman and I continued to read together with the same expected results. He didn't know why he didn't get it and neither did I, which I freely admitted. I consistently demanded that he not be loud and disruptive. When he was, I sent him to the office to sit out the rest of the class period. At least, then, my students and I were able to read in peace.

A Tempting Proposal

Eventually Herman managed to become less disruptive during SSR, spending much of his time looking at illustrated books of cars, or motorcycles, or people resplendent with tattoos. "Less disruptive" was still a far cry from nirvana, but we did achieve something approaching manageable. He continued to claim that he could learn more easily if he were buzzed and wanted to prove that to me by way of an experiment. He proposed that we work together after school, since he was not allowed to be under the influence of a controlled substance during school hours. He would leave campus for a very short time, get a quick buzz, then return for a reading lesson. Herman assured me he could be back at school by the time the bus left to take students home—that's how close and available his drug of choice was.

I'll confess that I was tempted to take it on. It *would* have been an interesting experiment. At the time though, I planned to teach for another fifteen years and needed to hold on to my teaching credentials.

The Mystery of Herman's Area of Reading Expertise

As far as I know, Herman never learned to attach meaning to the printed word. It was not until his second year at M.H.S. that a colleague and I realized there was a major exception to his comprehension problem. Herman could make sense of street signs, and he could follow a map! This was revealed to us when we set up a program that consisted mostly of field trips to places of historical interest, or to events where we could see examples of government in action.

Herman loved the class and was our most accurate navigator. Of course, he was still Herman, and the days when he was absent were easier and more productive than were the days when he showed up.

About five years after Herman turned eighteen and stopped coming to school, he came back to say hello. He still couldn't read. He was a roofer and claimed he got along just fine. Three years later, I heard he was in prison for manslaughter.

In the Midst of Failure, Remember the Successes

There are the kids who can't read because they can't afford glasses. Maybe the school can help, but usually it's a very lengthy process, sometimes longer than the students' time of enrollment. There are kids who work late into the night and can barely, if at all, stay awake. Hungover, stoned, addicted, abused, heartbroken, suicidal, hearing voices, pregnant, homeless, sick—all kinds of students walk through the doors of our classrooms. Some things we cannot fix, though we can never stop trying. In the midst of three A.M. tossing and turning over the Hermans in our realm, we must also keep in mind the readers like José, and Nancy, Gabriel and Estelle, and all the others who, because of our efforts and the efforts of others like us, are becoming lifelong readers, reaping the plenteous benefits of that practice.

Why Bother?

The "why bother" question hits hard at a Tuesday morning faculty meeting. About fifteen staff members are gathered in Room 5, waiting for the school counselor before we start the official meeting. We're talking about an upcoming school board election, a new lunch place nearby, a girl we suspect is pregnant, whatever . . .

Ms. B arrives a few minutes later, wearing a look we've seen all too often. Talking stops. She sighs, "Joe Ramirez. Drive by."

Ms. T, sitting beside me, puts her head down on the table, arms folded in front, as if preparing for a rainy day recess game of 7-Up. This is no game though.

We listen as Ms. B reveals the details: Gang related. Hit in the chest. Joe's cousin, too, is dead. All payback for a killing the previous month.

"I thought Joe wasn't involved in that. I thought he'd left the gang life," one of the less-seasoned teachers says.

Ms. B reminds him that none of this is rational.

Joe was seventeen, looked thirty, even acted thirty at times. At other times, he acted as if he were a two-year-old. He came to M.H.S. with a reputation of being one of the toughest of the tough, in the toughest local gang. (Because I don't want to give any gangs specific recognition, let's just abbreviate toughest local gang to TLG.) Joe was third-generation TLG.

At times his reputation worked toward keeping peace at school. He had clout with the wannabe gangbangers, the ones who most often have to prove something. If a fight were brewing, Joe only needed to say "not at school" and things calmed down. He could be funny, and charming, and was always quick to take a box of supplies from any teacher's hands and carry it into the classroom. He was into drugs, TLG, and all that goes with life on the street.

All of our students are "causes," but some loom larger than others. Joe was Ms. T's cause. He became her right-hand man for "Friday Night Live" events. He helped run the snack bar. He decided to work on math—something he'd given up on years ago. He was becoming one of those "turn-around" kids that offer us all hope. And he was dead.

Ms. B spoke of how best to handle the news with students, who all was thought to be involved, what repercussions might be in store.

When Ms. T eventually raised her head, her only comment was, "But he'd just finally learned his times tables."

Another Lost Cause

One of *my* causes was Luis. Although he, too, was affiliated with TLG, he was mostly a loner. His mother, who apparently had been his sole means of both financial and emotional support, had died two years earlier of breast cancer. He now lived with his grandmother in the house his mother had owned, but the grandmother was not up to the task.

Luis was bright, an avid reader, and a good writer. He loved the Tolkien books and took seriously my admonition to write from the heart. Much of what I knew about him came from his journal writings. He wrote of watching his mother struggle against cancer, of his last year with her, his sense of helplessness, and now his loneliness.

I arranged for Luis to attend a "grief group" at his old high school. He went once but decided he didn't need it. He had his own ways of dealing with grief.

His dream was to be an artist. So far, the only work he had shown publicly was on a freeway overpass, and the side wall of a bar not far from where he lived. He wanted more though and, according to Mr. N, our art teacher, Luis showed great potential.

For weeks at a time, Luis would be an exemplary student, working diligently and creatively, amassing credit quickly. Then, inexplicably, he would disappear. As Luis's advisor, one of my jobs was to call home. His grandmother was unaware that Luis hadn't been coming to school. She promised to check. The next day I called again. She told me that there was some mistake. Luis *had* been coming to school. He told her so.

We might hear that Luis and others from TLG had gone into rival gang territory and stirred up trouble, or that someone had seen him at a party. I would call the grandmother again and ask that she get Luis to school, and again be told that he *was* coming to school. I got help from the attendance clerk, and the counselor, but nothing *really* helped. Of course, we could turn his information over to the state's Attendance Review Board for stronger action, but he was only seven months away from eighteen, so would not be a priority.

In his own good time, Luis would return to school and again become an exemplary student. Early in April, Mr. N took Luis and three other promising students to visit a highly regarded art department at a nearby community college. Luis came back from that trip glowing with enthusiasm. He was determined to get into the art program he had visited, and both Mr. N and I set about helping Luis get things in order. High school graduation was within the realm of possibility, even though he was behind in credits.

The plan Luis and I agreed on was demanding, but it would assure him of meeting all requirements by mid-June. With Mr. N's guidance, Luis worked on rounding out his portfolio. Mr. N contacted the head of the art department and sang Luis's praises.

A Plan in Jeopardy

All went well until the middle of April when Luis disappeared for a week. Both Mr. N and I called the grandmother and tried to impress on her the importance of Luis being in school at this crucial time. "Tell Luis to come back to school," I would say to anyone with even the remotest connection to the talented, truant boy.

Luis's absence only lasted a week, which was less than previous disappearing acts, but greatly significant in light of his timeline. I bombarded him with questions of *why* had he been absent when he needed every school hour he could get to graduate on time, *what* was he thinking, *where* had he been; his answers were vague and unrevealing.

Beyond Death—a Mother's Influence

Although Luis didn't have much to say about what had kept him from school, his journal writings were slightly more revealing. There were times, he wrote, that he missed his mother so much he just had to take time for her. He felt her presence in his backyard, where she used to plant a big vegetable garden every year, and where there were several rosebushes that she had cared for with great love and tenderness. Even though the garden was now shabby, and Luis felt guilty for not taking care of it, he could always find his mother in the garden. She was, he wrote, very pleased about his plan for art school, and he wanted her to be proud of him. Luis tackled his remaining tasks with energy, and Mr. N and I were again hopeful.

I found his writing to be somewhat disconcerting, but what I've observed in others, and experienced in myself, is that the dead live on in the minds of the people who loved them. I thought that this was especially true for Luis. Although I generally consider journal writings to be confidential, I felt a need to mention Luis's talks with his mother to Ms. B. She called him in, ostensibly to talk with him about progress toward graduation, then led the conversation toward the grieving process. Ms. B's take on things was that Luis's "meetings" in the garden were a way for him to gather strength from the memory of his mother and that it was an important aspect of his healing.

Scholarship Decisions

Every June we gave twenty or so scholarships to graduates, or to students who were continuing their studies in a variety of ways including community colleges, the California Conservation Corps, and on-the-job training programs. The scholarships ranged in value from $25 to $500.

The annual faculty meeting at which we decided which students got which scholarships was a cross between a very intense tug-of-war and a peashooter fight. We all had causes, and we wanted our own causes to get the best scholarships. The year of Luis's graduation, Mr. N and I lobbied hard for him to get the $250 award. Peas were fired. Luis was too unpredictable. He didn't have the history with us that Brenda, another cause, had. We tugged hard on the rope. He was a kid with great talent and he knew exactly what his next step was. We shot a pea. Brenda was a sweet girl but she had no idea what was next for her. Another tug of the rope from Brenda's side—near perfect attendance. We shot the family support pea—Brenda had plenty of it, Luis had none.

Mr. N and I, along with a few other allies, prevailed. The $250 award went to Luis, with one of several $100 scholarships being designated for Brenda. The $500 scholarship was a no-contest decision for a girl who was everyone's cause. The others were tug-of-war, peashooter contests, but as always the decisions were made before dinnertime and we all breathed a sigh of relief that we wouldn't have to do *this* again for another year.

Luis Wins, and Loses

By the day of graduation, Luis had completed all of his necessary credits and had developed an impressive and well-balanced portfolio. His face shone with joy as he clutched his scholarship envelope and thanked Mr. N and me for all the help we had given. We, in turn, told Luis how much we had enjoyed working with him and urged him to keep in touch. He gave me a quick hug before getting on the bus and waved his scholarship envelope at me as the bus pulled away.

Mr. N, along with the principal and a few other designated staff, rode the bus that day too. There had been a rumor that a group of TLG rivals would be waiting at the bus stop where Luis and other TLGs got off. The plan was to thwart the rumored confrontation by having the bus driver change her usual route and let the TLGs off several blocks beyond the expected stop. This plan would probably have worked, except that when four girls without gang ties got off at the usual TLG place, several of the targeted TLG boys pushed out right behind them, ready to fight. Luis was among them. The bus driver radioed police and continued on her route. Mr. N told me later in the afternoon that his last vision of Luis was of him holding his scholarship check in one hand and hurling a broken beer bottle at one of the rivals with his other.

A week after school started in September an ex-student stopped by to tell us Luis had been found dead in his backyard. She said Luis had been sitting out there on a short stool, day and night, drinking for at least a week. He was wrapped in an Indian blanket, still sitting, stone cold dead when his grandmother found him.

We Bother Because We Must

Indeed, why bother? Because we have to. Because we can never predict who will be the turn-around student and who will meet an early death. And even for Luis, and Joe, and all of the others who come to an untimely end, we've offered hope and promise along the way. If it wasn't enough to save them, it was enough to brighten a few days. That's what I tell myself when the tossing and turning questions pop up in the dark, early morning hours. It's usually enough. (For more information about help for students, see TOTT: Getting Help for Troubled Students Who Can't and/or Won't Get with the Program, pp. 123–124.)

READERS ASK

Dear Ms. R,

Herman would never have been allowed to come back to my school if he'd been caught under the influence of a controlled substance because we have a zero tolerance policy for drugs, weapons, violent behavior. Don't you think all schools should have such policies?

Big on School Safety

Dear BOSS,

I think "zero tolerance" does a disservice to our most needy and disenfranchised students. Each case should be considered with all of its details and uncertainties. Even though Herman was not a success story, and admittedly was a trial to his teachers, I believe he was better off in school than roaming the streets without guidance or concern. Zero tolerance is an easy answer to very complex questions.

M.R.

Questions Only You Can Answer

○ Is there a student, or students, in my class who I've given up on?
○ Is there one more step to take that hasn't been taken?
○ How can I deal with the disappointments of teaching without losing sight of the successes?

Chapter Eight
Beware of Weapons of Mass Instruction

*. . . alas, to have no motive for learning to read other than to stay out
of trouble, to simply follow the rules of letters and sounds without a view
into the worlds that books represent, is a shame.*

Education Week, Peter Temes

How We Learn to Read

The majority of us learn to read in a way that is smooth and undramatic. Some learn to read in highly structured phonics programs. Some in whole language programs. Some learn to read at home, almost magically, before they even enter school. Most learn to read in a combination of ways. I learned with *Dick and Jane* in my school, but I also learned by following along in my grandmother's hymnal during congregational singing, and, soon after I started kindergarten, by sitting with my father in the evenings, sharing a beer and reading poems together. (See Appendix A if you want the rest of *that* story.)

I recently conducted a small informal study in which I asked friends, neighbors, and a variety of email acquaintances if they could remember *learning* to read. Most could only remember knowing how to read somewhere between the ages of five and seven, but the process of how they reached that knowledge was lost to them. A few offered specific experiences ranging from being rapped on the hand with a ruler if they misread a word, to happily noticing the connections between letters and sounds through *Hop on Pop* and other Dr. Seuss favorites.

One person remembered his sense of shame at not learning to read when he was supposed to and the coping devices he used to keep from being found out. It wasn't until he was in high school and an English teacher took a particular interest in him that he learned to read in spite of his then undiagnosed dyslexia. This man recently retired from teaching, and later directing, classes in Special Education. He is still in contact with his high school English teacher, who is now ninety-eight years old.

The One-Size-Fits-All Fallacy

As I continue asking the "how did you learn to read" question of people ranging in age from eight to eighty, the one constant is that there is no constant. The one-size-fits-all approach to teaching reading is parallel to the one-size-fits-all pair of pants at Macy's. "One size fits all" usually means, "one size doesn't fit anyone," at least not very well.

The whole language/phonics wars are a constant source of amazement to me. Will your struggling reader learn to read better if he receives phonics instruction every day? Sure. He will be much better equipped to look at a word and figure out how to say it, although he may not improve in comprehension and will probably not be imbued with the joy of reading.

Will your struggling reader learn to read better if she is steeped in a whole language program every day? Sure. She will find meaning and interest in stories through the printed word, although she may have trouble deciphering a new, polysyllabic word.

Will these struggling readers learn to read better with a program that combines whole language and phonics? Am I missing something here, or is that not the pinnacle of a no-brainer question?

SSR and Low-Level Readers?

But what does the whole language/phonics debate have to do with SSR teens? The average and above average teen reader is unlikely to be caught in this debate, since they've already learned to read by one method or another, or, we could hope, by a mix of methods. For those who have not yet learned to read well enough to test somewhere near their grade level, and for ELL (English Language Learners) who are not yet proficient readers of English, the debate rages over how best to move them along.

Does SSR work for these students? That's a question addressed by Janice L. Pilgreen in *The SSR Handbook*. She used five ESL (English as a Second Language) students as subjects for a study that measured improvement in comprehension, greater enjoyment of reading, increased reading for pleasure beyond school, belief in themselves as better readers, and the use of a wider range of sources for pleasure reading. Considerable improvement occurred in all five of these areas. Reading comprehension showed gains of fifteen months over a period of sixteen weeks, with equally impressive gains in the four other categories.

Many high schools offer what we once called "remedial reading" for low-scoring freshmen. Now such classes are more likely to be labeled "developmental reading," or something jazzier, but whatever they're called, their purpose is to bring low-level readers to the point where they can read well enough to function in academic subjects throughout high school. What we know from programs, such as SAFARI, Janice Pilgreen's SSR classes, and scores of others, is that SSR, combined with other instruction and activities, is highly effective for such readers.

I often hear from teachers who use SSR with Special Education students. Recently Michele Ritt, a teacher in Madison, Wisconsin, sent me a stack of letters from her students. Some letters were addressed to characters in my novel *Baby Help* and some were addressed to me. All were interesting and thought-provoking. Michele's accompanying letter said, in part: "My students all have learning differences. You [your books] provide a connection with them and the valuable experience that they *can* read and *can* love to read . . ."

Frightening Trends

SSR obviously works on several levels. What frightens me, though, are the trends I see in moving toward weapons of mass instruction—weapons that can't possibly hit the target of offering a balanced reading program. Although I decry the narrowness of educators who are zealous believers in phonics only, or whole language only, they seem uncharacteristically broad in comparison to the "scripted learning" camp.

A superintendent in a northern California school district was recently reported to be such a true believer of his district's newly ensconced scripted learning program that he wants "to walk from classroom to classroom at the same grade level, with no interruption of instruction. I want to be able to hear the next sentence when I enter the next room. I want no interruption in continuity."

Grousing

Janice Auld, president of the North Sacramento Education Association says, "A trained monkey could do this program. . . . It's humiliating and demeaning. In my teacher's guide it says, 'Put your book on your lap. Put the card on the table. Show children this. Their response will be that.'"

Scripted learning programs are now finding their way into middle schools and high schools. What would that have done for José, the "reading will lead lives" guy from Chapter 3? He might actually be better able to divide a word into syllables than he can now, but would he be writing a book? And although his book may have misspellings, it is a life-changing experience for him. Misspellings are easy to correct. Not being guided toward a lifelong reading habit isn't.

Highly Structured Reading Programs Are No Substitute for SSR

While I'm grousing, I'd like to offer a minor grouse about highly structured reading programs (HSRP). These programs rely on the theory that students are more motivated to read if they are rewarded for correct answers on comprehension checks and if they can chart their progress as they advance in reading levels. Tests and tracking are computerized, which is also a draw for today's students. The best-known program of this kind is Accelerated Reader, and many teachers find it to be a very effective tool.

I won't go so far as to label HSRPs as "weapons of mass instruction." They offer a choice of books and provide time for silent reading. The immediate assessment of progress is reassuring to both students and teachers. However, many of the elements of an effective SSR program are missing. Choices are limited to a range of grade levels. There can be flexibility within these designations, but generally the program does not allow for the 7.3 level student who wants to revisit Dr. Seuss or *Tales of a Fourth Grade Nothing*. Even if the teacher is flexible enough to allow this, there is the problem of lost points, which often causes such students to deny their own knowledge or instinct of what they most want to be reading, and to sell out for the sake of points.

If a student finds a "hit" book and then wants to read everything else by that author, he may be frustrated to find that the author's other books are not on the HSRP list. It *is* possible for teachers to make their own tests, but they may not be able or willing to add yet another task to their already burgeoning to-do list.

As useful as HSRPs may be, many of the practices and activities do not translate to a lifelong reading habit. When I visit my comfy, independent bookstore and see a book that I've *got* to read, I don't go to the computer and check to see if it's in my reading-level range. I doubt that you do either.

Free Choice in Books Is a Necessity, Not a Luxury

Here's what worries me about a HSRP. Estelle, from Chapter 4, could not have read *Telling* even if it had been on the HSRP program. It was way above her reading level. She would have missed hearing the angel whisper "grow, grow." Who knows how much longer she would have carried her burden in silence?

José, from Chapter 3, also would not have been allowed to read his first "hit" book because it would have been deemed too difficult for him.

The HSRP book list would not have included a wonderful but not well-known book that elicited this letter from a student a few years after she left M.H.S.:

> Dear Mrs. R,
>
> In a few more years, when everything becomes hazy and I can't remember the story and why I liked it so much, I am going to reread The Bookmakers Daughter. This book was very influential and it felt very sincere and original when I read it— when you led me to it in high school. I think it was one of my first very wonderful experiences in reading.
>
> I had read other interesting books before this one, but this seemed to be a definitive, resounding experience for me unlike any other I had had. And it perhaps, more than the book itself, and actually the moment sparkles to me still because I believe that the book triggered in me my then nascent love of language and the resplendent permanence of words encased forever in books. Abbott's book was one of the first I read slowly and carefully, relishing her every thought.
>
> W.W.

Momentarily Setting Aside My Missionary Zeal for SSR

A year or so ago I took an adjunct position at a local community college, teaching a few hours a week in the Reading Center. My students ranged in age from eighteen to sixty-two, and their reading level range was equally broad. Many were recently promoted out of ESL classes into Basic Reading Skills, which was one of several course offerings available through the Reading Center. They were trying to improve their English skills to the point where they could manage vocational or standard academic courses. Others were working toward entry into English 1A. Some drop-ins worked on essay analysis as part of a more advanced English class in which they were enrolled. Many had physical difficulties, seizures, cerebral palsy, and other problems not so easily labeled. Reading Center work was totally individualized and highly structured, centering on specific skills with a challenge to students to increase the difficulty of their work after each completed segment. There was a packet that offered the possibility of earning credit by reading a novel, but it was seldom mentioned when teachers were discussing work possibilities with students.

How would I take to such a program, given my penchant for Sustained Silent Reading, and my reluctance to have the main purpose of reading to be to simply find the answer, as happens with comprehension workbooks?

One of the aspects of teaching at alternative high schools that never lost its charm for me was the diversity of the students who walked through my classroom door. Reading Center students were not all that different from the M.H.S. bunch—just older and more highly motivated. I loved working with them, and I could see that the specific skills approach was of value to their learning processes.

When I signed on at the community college, I was determined not to let my missionary zeal for SSR keep me from doing justice to the basic skills coursework as it was set up. I did that, going from student to student, working with them on how to find the main idea in a paragraph or longer article, giving them extra practice in how to determine fact versus opinion, and checking various vocabulary-building exercises. Because of the range and quantity of individualized materials, there was much for me to learn, and I did my homework. But I couldn't keep my own strong instincts out of it.

Promoting Reading for Pleasure Amid Basics

I often suggested the novel packet as homework, and set about helping the student find a book he/she might like. Between the small classroom library, the college library, and my own stash, I did manage to get a few students on the reading-for-pleasure bandwagon. Mostly though, they were working and/or raising families in addition to attending school, and they wanted the security the basic skills work brought them.

Although the Reading Center work was a step away from the core of reading for me, it was effective in many ways and the variety of materials allowed for some choice according to areas of interest. But . . .

One man came in each period, got his folder, took his place at a computer, and began work on a highly structured, piece-by-piece computer program. At first I worked with others and left L.R. to my extraordinarily overqualified aide. I knew nothing of the computer program except that even from across the room I could tell I didn't like it.

Again, the Student Educates the Teacher

After a few weeks, when I did deign to sit beside L.R. to see what was going on, I was appalled! The questions were so poorly worded that even I couldn't figure out what the answer was supposed to be. If L.R. chose a wrong answer to a question, say "Identify the topic sentence of this paragraph," he would get a beep, and then a garbled explanation of what was wrong with his chosen answer. The vocabulary was a bit more straightforward and at least was tied to the text, but overall the program could have entered the Worst Computer Reading Program Ever Devised competition and won in all categories. Still . . .

The man loved it. As I girded my loins each class period and joined L.R. who was identifying a badly worded question at the loathsome blinking cursor, I learned more of his story. He was probably in his mid-forties, medium height, with a very compact build. I guessed his muscles were earned on the job rather than at a fitness club. He always wore a baseball cap and was neatly dressed in clean jeans and a tee shirt that bore no logo. He was quiet, but pleasant.

At Forty-Four, Finally a Reader

He told me it was his third semester at the Reading Center, and he'd learned to read on the computer. Forty-four, and he'd just learned to read. I asked if he'd ever worked with any of the other materials in the classroom.

"Nope. Just the computer."

I asked if he read at home. He told me he read the little strip that goes across the bottom of the TV. He used to not understand anything it said. Now he got most of it.

He fought tears as he told me of his relief at finally being able to read. He talked of being passed from one class to the next, from elementary school on, even though both he and his teachers knew he wasn't learning. As long as he was quiet, he said, no one even noticed him. When L.R. was a senior in high school, one of his teachers *did* notice. Together they set a goal that L.R. would be able to read the newspaper by the time he left high school. It didn't happen, but at least *one* teacher had tried. He said how much he appreciated the Reading Center and that he would never have learned to read without it.

I took another look at the computer program, thinking I must have missed something, but no, it was the same mess it had been when I first took a look.

A Drug That Helped—Maybe Herman Was Right

After a few months of checking in with L.R. each period, he offered another emotion-filled revelation: The drug Depacote had made life worth living.

Before that he couldn't settle down or focus on any one thing for more than a few minutes. He sometimes heard voices and the intensity of his anger frightened him. It was probably Depacote that made it possible for him to concentrate on reading he said, and that maybe if he'd taken it as a kid he could have learned to read in school. He doesn't understand why people are so antidrugs for kids with problems. Did he hear voices in school? No, but he would have to count the holes in the ceiling tiles rather than pay attention to what was going on in the classroom.

So . . . I had my rigid biases challenged. A drug and a very poorly written computer program turned L.R. into a reader. Although I don't recommend it, I can't deny it. If I can quote my granny once again, "There's more than one way to skin a cat."

More Happy Accidents

Even though the computer had been effective for L.R., and he loved it, I couldn't come to terms with his never opening a book. I asked if he'd ever read a book. He hadn't. Would he like to? He didn't think so. But we made a deal. He would try reading a book, just as an experiment. I wanted to get Gary Paulsen's *Hatchet*, a book I thought might appeal to L.R. because I knew he liked to camp. The library only had one Gary Paulsen novel though, and that was *Crossing*. I gave it a try. When I asked the next day, L.R. said he'd read the first chapter and it was pretty good. Then he proceeded to give a detailed account of what he'd read. He finished it in about two weeks and told me the whole story. I asked if he'd like another book and he said he'd try one. I decided to go to a different library to look for *Hatchet*.

It was time for me to leave for school the next day when I realized I'd not done anything about finding the book. I was determined not to show up empty handed so I did a quick search of my shelves. Nothing looked right. With a sinking feeling, I grabbed Joan Bauer's *Squashed* and left. Joan Bauer has a wonderful sense of humor, and her book was written on a level that L.R. could manage, but it's about a high school girl who raises pumpkins. I expected it to be a bust. I handed it to L.R. anyway, telling him I'd find something else if he didn't like it.

I expected him to hand the book back to me when I saw him next. Instead, he told me it was about a girl who raised pumpkins and wanted to grow the winning biggest pumpkin for the state fair. L.R. had a look of wonder as he told me this girl used Big Max seeds, the same kind of seeds he used. He showed me the empty Big Max seed packet he was using for a bookmark. He said the girl in the story used her own secret formula of buttermilk and orange crush to make her pumpkin grow big, and he was going to try it. I, too, had a sense of wonder as I heard L.R.'s version of the story—one of those little book-matching wins that are unpredictable but delightful.

On the way home other, more momentous, serendipitous events came to mind—running into F in the market, meeting up with Gloria Miklowitz in a writing class, carpooling with a woman who would eventually become my scriptwriting partner and who would be instrumental in getting my *Too Soon for Jeff* novel produced as an after school special. We were both nominated for an Emmy for that scriptwriting task—all because of a carpool.

Less significant happy coincidences also came to mind—meeting an old school chum on an overseas flight, having a letter to a friend pass hers in the mail after neither of us had written for two years. I thanked the universe for happy accidents, big and small, as I pulled into the market parking lot, wondering who I might meet up with.

The Lifelong Reading Key

It was not easy to maintain a writing/speaking schedule and stay responsible to the Reading Center. I left after my second semester there, but my experiences had presented me with a valuable reality check and reminded me that there are indeed many ways to teach reading. Even so, I remain convinced that the greatest gift I offered L.R., and the several other Basic Skills students who took the bait, was the key to the door of a lifelong reading habit. It is the gift I want to continue giving. So now I'm off to write the next teen novel, which I hope will become another "first book I ever read" experience for some unsuspecting reluctant reader.

My wish for you, teachers, writers, readers of all ilk, is that you may be blessed with serendipitous events, hear the voice of the whispering angel, and trust (except when on bridges and in high buildings) that when you jump the net will appear.

READERS ASK

Dear Ms. R,

Now that you've been reminded that there are a whole variety of ways to teach reading, would you include some of the basic skills practice books that were used at the community college in an SSR program?

See a Need for Basics

Dear See,

No way. I see a need for basics, too, but not in an SSR program. Remember, SSR is working toward a lifelong reading for pleasure habit in an adult world. Classtime other than SSR might be used for basic skills, phonics reminders, spelling, and a host of other reading-related activities. The key here is reading-related, rather than pure, unadulterated reading.

M.R.

Dear Ms. R,

I've been using a scripted learning program with my ninth-grade developmental readers for the past two years. I love it and so do they. We all know exactly what we're doing and when we're doing it. Their test scores have improved and so have my yearly evaluations. What's wrong with that?

Scripted and Proud

Dear S&P,

I sincerely doubt that all twenty-five to thirty students in your classroom are at the exact same level of understanding, yet they're being treated as if that were the case. Are they learning the joy of reading, or the joy of repetition in unison? Which is the more important goal? Do you ever get bored with it?

M.R.

Questions Only You Can Answer

○ Am I relying on highly structured programs because I feel more secure doing something that's set rather than using my own insight and creativity to reach the diversity of the individuals in my classroom?

○ How did *I* learn to read?

Chapter Nine
From Teacher to Writer

—a woman must have money and a room of her own
if she is to write fiction.
A Room of One's Own, Virginia Woolf

—a man, too.
Not Yet Published Addendum to Virginia Woolf, Marilyn Reynolds

The Price of Eggs?

You may ask, "What's this 'teacher to writer' business doing in a book about help-ing reluctant readers develop a lifelong reading habit?" Or, as my granny used to say whenever one strayed from the topic at hand, "What's that got to do with the price of eggs?"

For one thing, the broader world needs the insights of grounded educators to offer a realistic portrayal of the state of education. The prolific pundits who present themselves as experts, even though they've not seen the inside of a public school classroom since their own graduation from high school, wield more influence over public opinion than is to be desired. The more the public hears from real teachers, the better our chances are of garnering intelligent support for public education. My hope for this chapter is that it will stimulate your latent writing itch, and that you can add a touch of realism to the zillions of words that float around education issues.

When I started this book I expected to rely exclusively on my teaching life for reading-related experiences and observations. But it soon became obvious that I couldn't separate teaching from writing, or writing from teaching, and that to try was a false exercise. How could I not talk about the increased awareness gained when students read of themselves and their school in one of my essays published in a national newspaper? Or of the greater understanding of literary analysis that occurred when students critiqued early drafts of my books? Or the influence my persistent rewriting efforts had on the typical reluctant writer's innate aversion to work beyond first drafts?

Another aspect of the "price of eggs" question concerns conversations with teachers, librarians, counselors, and administrators at schools and conferences over this past decade. Many of these folks, especially teachers, express a strong desire to tell their unique stories, some related to education, others to the broad spectrum of creative writing possibilities.

Reality Checks from In-the-Field Educators

It should be no surprise that English teachers, reading teachers, and librarians are writers, closet or otherwise. We were drawn to our fields through a love of books, which is, at the core, a love of stories. And, oh man, do we have stories to tell! And it is extremely important that we tell our stories. If we leave it to high-level bureaucrats to pontificate on their skewed versions of an educational utopia, where 100 percent of all students test above the fiftieth percentile, then it is no wonder the general public thinks that the quality of education can be measured by how well students can bubble in the acceptable "a," "b," "c," or "d" on a printed form provided by a national testing service.

It is of utmost importance that teachers offer reality checks to the broader public, and one of the most efficient and effective ways to do that is through publication of letters and opinion pieces in newspapers and other periodicals that reach a wide readership.

Help from Teachers Who Write

Teachers who write can also provide clarity and perspective on the classroom. As I struggled with the reality of students who couldn't and/or wouldn't conform to a standard classroom setting, I did not turn to scholarly books about education theory. Instead, I devoured books by teachers who faced difficulties similar to my own: *Up the Down Staircase* by Bel Kaufman, *The Way It S'pozed to Be* and *How to Survive in Your Native Land* by James Herndon, *The Water Is Wide* by Pat Conroy, and a number of others (see References).

Such books were invaluable to me. They depicted the realities of teaching the supposedly unteachable in the midst of bureaucratic absurdities, and they did so with great humor and honesty. These writers didn't offer much in the way of "how-tos," but the strength of their examples gave me the courage to stray from the traditional authoritarian approach to education in which I was steeped.

Through honest dialog with colleagues, and through reflections on the writings of such teachers as Kaufman, Herndon, and Conroy, it became more and more apparent to me that I must recognize the individuality of each student, and teach accordingly. But *how* could I manage *that*? A large piece of the answer to that question was a Sustained Silent Reading program, which respected the reader and offered him/her a full partnership in the processes of learning.

I am forever grateful to the thousands of writers who, over the years, have awakened me to thoughts and worlds beyond my ken. I would have been lost without them. With that in mind, I urge those of you with the desire to write to get started, and those of you who are already started I urge to stay with it—to offer others the power of your unique stories. Which brings us to ask again, "But *how* could I manage *that*?" I can't really answer that question for you. However, from talking with teachers who struggle to find a way to fit writing into their already too busy lives, I know they are hungry to hear how others manage it. I expect you may share that hunger, and I can offer a light repast.

The Hard Way

I started writing a little while still teaching a lot. Slowly, over a period of several years, the balance shifted to writing a lot and teaching a little. Here's how my teaching/writing practices evolved.

In keeping with a propensity to do things the hard way, I waited to start college until I had two daughters, ages eighteen months and three years, and was divorced. The first year at a community college I took a creative writing class because it met my two requirements for choosing any class—it fit the girls' babysitting schedule and it offered English credit.

I'd not been a good student since the sixth grade, so I entered college filled with doubt and uncertainty regarding my academic abilities. When I saw A grades and complimentary comments on returned creative writing papers, I was astonished. Often my papers were read in class and were well received by younger classmates. Most of what I wrote then, when given an "anything you want" assignment, was in the style of, but I'm afraid not the quality of, syndicated humorist Erma Bombeck, who also took her material from everyday life.

I was awarded the creative writing prize for the semester, and my work was included in the college literary magazine. The advisor for the magazine encouraged me to become involved with that community of writers and, although the possibility intrigued me, anything that would require more hours of babysitting was not a possibility.

At Cal State Los Angeles (now California State University at Los Angeles), I continued to enjoy writing and to be recognized as a strong writer, though I never even imagined writing professionally.

Leap and the Net Will Appear

After my divorce settlement I had $1,800 in cash, plus a court-ordered monthly stipend of $200 in child support. I decided that the $1,800, coupled with child support and a part-time job, would see me through one year of college. With sweaty palms and pounding heart, I took the leap. I quit my low-paying but steady job and enrolled as a full-time student. At the end of that year, I received two scholarships totaling $500, which got me through the next semester. One of the scholarships was reinstated each semester, a small but much-needed financial help, and a huge lift to my sense of confidence. My parents let us stay with them for two years. Government loans picked up some slack, and we eked by.

When I graduated from Cal State with a B.A. in English, my daughters had never been to the dentist, nor had I for six years. We had no health insurance and were living very close to the edge, month by month. My first year in college I had discovered that my younger daughter, Cindi, was severely hard of hearing. She had been wearing loaner hearing aids since the age of two, but time on the loaners had run out: I had to come up with a considerable sum of money to purchase new hearing aids.

So . . . let's see. Struggling writer? Teacher? No contest. It was *so* no contest that the struggling writer question never entered my conscious mind. The teaching decision was made with a pound of idealism and a ton of practicalities, and although that may sound unexciting, it turned out to be anything but.

Serendipity at the Piano

Whatever discretionary funds I had from my first teaching paycheck went to the local dentist. But with my second paycheck, I could finally afford to secure the piano lessons that my oldest daughter, Sharon, had long coveted. She loved learning to play the piano and, within a few short weeks, she fell in love with Mike, her piano teacher. I fell, a few weeks after Sharon did, and Cindi followed suit.

Within six months, Mike and I married. The girls were nine and seven at the time. Included in Mike's bonus package were also an aging Cocker Spaniel and a pesky orange cat. Slightly less than two years later our son, Matt, was born. He was adored beyond reason by us all, except for the cat, who was indifferent.

From Rejection to a Room of My Own to Publication

During a short new-motherhood gap in my teaching career, I took advantage of nap times and wrote what I thought was a perfect story for MS. magazine. I received a nice note back, but no sale. I then sent *Redbook* a "Mom's True Story" about the joys and sorrows of raising a deaf child. This also got a note and no sale. And then I was back to the classroom.

Balancing teaching responsibilities, raising a family, building a healthy second marriage, and taking on the occasional political cause kept me happily hopping. For the next decade, my writing skills were devoted to notes to the kids reminding them to feed the dog and transfer the clothes from the washer to the drier. Those notes, plus copious shopping and to-do lists were it, until I took a sabbatical to complete work on a master's degree in Reading Education. When I finished that degree, with a little time to spare, I gave myself the gift of a creative writing class at Pacific Oaks, a small private college in Pasadena.

It was not until both of my daughters were gone from home that I expanded my writing practices beyond the confines of bossy notes and lists. I turned their bedroom into a workspace, just for me. I gathered my most-loved books from places scattered throughout the house and shelved them in the "new" room. I put my typewriter (yes, typewriter) on a long wooden table and picked up a couple of orange crates to use for files. It was fun putting it together, and it meant I would no longer have to clear projects off the dining room table before we could sit down to dinner.

I understand that when Judith Guest wrote *Ordinary People*, she did it in the wee small hours of the morning, her writing tablet resting on the washing machine. She and others like her, who must write anywhere, no matter what, have my greatest respect and admiration. Me, I needed that quiet space, away from the TV, safe from household distractions—that "room of her own" made famous by Virginia Woolf.

So, equipped with my room and a little time, my thoughts wandered toward writing. It turned out that the class I took at Pacific Oaks had a strong focus on nourishing our creative sides, a side long neglected during my busy, practical life. One of the many creative exercises we did in class kindled long-buried scenes from my childhood, and I wrote without pause of my remembrances of the sudden disappearance of a Japanese family during World War II, when all West Coast Japanese were "interned" (See Appendix C).

The Thrill of Publication

At the encouragement of the teacher, I typed out the essay and sent it off to the *Los Angeles Times*. When the Op-Ed editor called a few weeks later to say they wanted to use it, I was elated. "It's really good," she told me. She apologized that they only paid $100. My husband, Mike, and I had long since spent the $100 in celebration before the check actually arrived.

When the essay appeared, I got calls from people I hadn't heard from in years. I got letters from people, both Japanese and others, who lived through that time, and I was struck by the awareness that my words had meant something to so many readers.

Hit and Miss Essays

The long-dormant idea that I might like to write rose to full consciousness, and for several years I wrote personal essays and sent them out cold to newspapers and magazines. I wrote about family life, and education. I wrote about a neighborhood kidnapping and the end of an era with the closing of a famed department store. I was hired to write a weekly column for a local newspaper. I loved the process and discipline of it, though I turned every column into a more demanding task than it needed to be.

After a few months, the local paper that was publishing "Reynolds Rap" folded, and I was back to sending things out, hit and miss. My guess is that I hit with about half of what I wrote, though I didn't keep statistics.

Several published essays told of my experiences in alternative education, and often offered my assessment of broader issues within our district and state. In writing about budget cuts, I linked that to the services that would no longer be available to students—no nurse to advise and follow up on the student with daily stomach pains; no counselor to help the suicidal student.

It surprised me that many people who read my essays were so shocked by the effects of budget cuts on the students who most needed help. Many readers were also unaware of the plight of at-risk students. Who can blame them? I, too, was unaware of the plight of at-risk students until I began working with them.

Begging You, Please

For you teachers/writers, here is my plea. Write about education. Of course, write the Great American Novel and poetry that makes hearts sing. But *please*, spend a fraction of your writing efforts on your school conditions and experiences and on the broader implications for the state of the nation and the world. If what the general public reads in newspapers and magazines comes mainly from politicians and high-level bureaucrats, it is no wonder there is so little regard for public education.

The "raise the standards" banner is compelling, but the public has little understanding of what is lost when the major classroom focus is on improving test scores. *You* can offer a balanced view—a much-needed reality check. *Your* particular insights are needed.

A very important fringe benefit of your writing will be the effect it has on your students. It gives them credibility. Some see that they are important enough to write about, and that others will read about them and their school situations. It gives you credibility and belies the offensive but popular adage that those who can, do, and those who can't, teach. More important, your writing raises the level of reflection.

More Serendipity

Besides personal essays, I also wrote some short fiction. One of my stories was published in a well-regarded literary magazine, but the fiction was even more of a miss than the essays; I wanted more. I wanted to boost the ratio of works published over works yellowing in a drawer.

In a move that can only be defined as serendipitous, I signed up for a community college extension class titled Writing for Publication. It met one evening a week and was taught by Gloria Miklowitz, a highly respected and prolific author of Young Adult (YA) fiction. She offered a wealth of knowledge regarding possible markets. Several others in the class were further along the publishing road than I, so there was much to be learned.

Within a matter of weeks, Gloria was urging me to try a YA novel. My attitude at the time was, "I work with teens all day, why would I write about them all night and on weekends?" But the seed was planted. Gloria's urgings, plus my need to have more truly realistic fiction in the classroom, got me started on *Telling*, and one book led to another. As I mentioned in Chapter 1, I now have written eight realistic teen fiction books—thanks to the goddess for serendipity.

Blending Teaching and Writing

Most of my teaching "innovations" have been a result of happy accidents rather than careful planning, and offering my own writing for student appraisal was such an accident. With the first chapters of *Telling* (working title, *Don't Let Him Catch You Alone*), I realized I needed a critique group with demographics other than the mostly middle-class, white, female members of my two writing groups.

I decided to try *Telling* on my students. They were quick to let me know they didn't like one of the phrases I'd used—I don't think it was as bad as "gee whiz," but it might have been. They offered a number of alternatives. I reminded them that I was hoping the book would get published and that using the "f" word on page two might get in the way. They brainstormed other words and we ended up with a good substitution. Other than my antiquated phrase, they liked the first chapter and wanted to hear more.

Somewhere around Chapter 3, I began to feel guilty that I was exploiting my students for selfish purposes. SSR time was still sacred, but other assignments had taken a backseat to the reading of *Telling*. Yet, the class that was reading my embryonic novel entered the room with more enthusiasm than was exhibited prior to *Telling*. If I didn't have a new chapter for them, they nagged me to get busy. They offered suggestions about what I should write next, usually along the lines of who should kick Fred Sloane's butt, although occasionally someone came up with a more sophisticated idea. Here's the thing though—the students were developing a critical sense, using literary terms, analyzing character and motivation. And, they were paying attention to the specifics of language use.

Literary Analysis for Real Life

It was much more real to them to talk about characters who might still change in one way or another, according to their suggestions, than to talk about what a character in a book might have done differently, or to predict what would happen in a book that was already in print. What difference would their prediction make in *Of Mice and Men*? Ah, but the as-yet unpublished *Telling*—*those* predictions might actually make a difference in the outcome of the story. This was critiquing for real life, so I stopped feeling guilty.

The first six books I wrote were with the help of M.H.S. students. Not that I gave their insights more credence than my own. Some of their comments were bizarre. One student insisted that a spaceship filled with aliens should come kidnap Fred Sloan and get him out of Cassie's life. In spite of such capricious comments though, I found much that was valuable in student responses.

Several times my teen critics saved me from some anachronistic detail; one time in particular remains lodged in my memory. I was reading a section of *Detour for Emmy* in which Emmy, sleep deprived and still recovering from giving birth, gets up in the middle of the night to change the baby and give her a bottle. After putting a clean diaper on Rosie, Emmy takes the dirty one into the bathroom, rinses it in the toilet, and deposits it in the diaper pail.

"She wouldn't do that!" one of the girls yelled.

"Nobody uses cloth diapers anymore!" another chimed in.

"Haven't you ever heard of Pampers?"

I could only laugh.

"You better fix that," the girl with the Pampers question said.

I did. Certainly I'd heard of Pampers and had seen all manner of folk using disposable diapers. But in writing that section, my unconscious mind had pulled me back to a time when I was a young mother changing my infant daughter's diaper, rinsing it, and dropping it into what would now be an antique diaper pail. I'm grateful to those students for saving me the embarrassment of cloth diapers in this world of disposables.

Expanding the Field of Teen Critics

When we moved from southern California four hundred miles north to the Sacramento area, I left behind my captive literary critics and had to find new sources for teen readers. This I managed through a nearby continuation high school, and through teachers and librarians I met at conferences who would say, "I've got a student who I think would really like to read your manuscript."

Recently, I've been in touch with some of my manuscript readers through email. This is a very convenient and efficient means of getting reader responses, but it can't totally replace the face-to-face interaction I've come to rely on.

It scares me to think of writing a book for teens without teen critics. "Gee whiz," and cloth diapers, and who knows what else might sneak by. Such oversights would be distressing to one who claims to write *realistic* teen fiction.

Much of my contact with teens now takes place when I go to middle or high schools as a visiting author. The questions I get from these students force me to clarify some aspects of my writing life that might otherwise, happily, remain unconscious.

Priming the Inspiration Pump

Invariably there is a question about where I get my inspiration. I respond that much of my inspiration comes from letters I get from readers like themselves, letting me know that my books have made a difference. That much is true, but there is a more mystical side to "inspiration" that defies explanation.

Of course, if I waited for inspiration before I showed up at my computer, no more books or essays would ever be published. I would be back to the shopping and to-do lists. Dreams, a chance remark, something from the newspaper or a magazine may kick off an idea. I *suppose* that's a form of inspiration. Mostly though, inspiration comes as a surprise, when I'm sitting at my computer and a character shows up on the page, unplanned, and has his way with my story. Or when the perfect phrase comes to me to enrich what might have been a dull piece of dialog.

Writing Groups

Another possibility for inspiration comes from interacting with other writers. After the Pacific Oaks class was over, I received a postcard from one of the teachers, saying that another member of that class wanted to start a writing group, and asking if she could pass my phone number on to that person. I said yes, and so did others.

Six of us gathered to talk about the possibility. We set up tentative guidelines and decided to meet again in another month. The person who initiated the group did not continue, but the rest of us did. At the time, I was the only published writer, with one measly essay notch on my belt. Since then, everyone has published work—a book that started out as a short family history and turned into a wonderful, full-length biography; a TV script; many personal essays; children's stories and poetry. We published a collection of essays, stories, and poetry and have performed our work at a variety of soirees and coffeehouses. We remain a writing "group" to this day, although we are now only a trio. We lost one much-loved member to cancer and another to dementia, but our influence on one another over the decades continues and is immeasurable.

A Crooked Path

Another question I'm often asked at school visits is, "Did you always know you wanted to be a writer?"

I confess that I hadn't a clue. My first career goal, at the age of three or so, was to be a cowboy. I wanted to ride an old paint and sing "yippee ti yi yo, get along little doggies" out on the open range.

With the advent of World War II, I wanted to be a sergeant in the army, something along the lines of a John Wayne hero. In junior high school, I looked over my friend's shoulder and wrote, as she had, "stewardess" and "nurse" on a form that asked about future plans. I would have been completely unsuited to either of those tasks, but I didn't know what else to write. "Teacher" would have been out of the question, no matter what my friends chose, since by that time I was entrenched in the antischool attitude I'd maintained from sixth through twelfth grade.

"Writer?"—I hardly knew such people existed. As much as I loved books and reading, I had not yet given thought to where the stories came from. I could name a few writers, all of whom should make any English teacher blush with shame over her early choices of trite and insipid materials. Even being able to name authors though didn't mean that I grasped the idea of a person actually putting words on paper and having those words transformed into a book.

I have, at times, been envious of the person who knows from birth exactly what they want to be—doctor, writer, teacher, and so on. It seems a much more efficient way to live one's life. In the same way I've at times been envious of the writer who knows at the beginning of his/her book how it's going to end and what's going to happen along the way. People with life plans. Writers who work from outlines.

It has taken me half a lifetime to figure out what I most want to do, just as it takes me half a book to figure out what story I'm really writing. But, in spite of my occasional envy of those who've found a straighter path, I wouldn't trade places. The joy of happy accidents and serendipitous meetings is well worth the crooked path. Of course, happy accidents must be coupled with intention.

READERS ASK

Dear Ms. R,

My wife thinks I should be spending all of my "free" time with the kids—soccer games, dance lessons, board games, bedtime stories—how can I write when every spare minute is taken?

Thwarted Writer

Dear T.W.,

Make a plan. It must be fair and it must accommodate the realistic needs of your children. Be sure that however much time you set aside for yourself is balanced by time your wife has for herself. Maybe you start with thirty minutes each morning, before the kids are up. Or maybe you and your wife trade off bedtime responsibilities so that you get an hour one evening and she gets an hour the next. Write during that time—even if your inspiration gauge is below empty. Respect your plan.

M.R.

Dear Ms. R,

I sent a manuscript out once and it came back with a form rejection, without even the courtesy of a signature. My self-esteem plummeted, I was depressed for months. It frightens me to even think of trying again.

Defeated, Dejected, Discouraged

Dear 3D,

How about switching to Determined, Diligent, and Disciplined? Jack London collected 644 rejections in five years. He kept sending out manuscripts and became one of the best-known and well-paid writers of his time. How about a goal of a mere 300 rejections before you give up?

M.R.

Questions Only You Can Answer

○ Am I willing to work through the hard times, when ideas are scarce and the weather's nice?

○ What distractions do I succumb to during the time I set aside for writing?

○ Am I willing to do the necessary drudge work of polishing and repolishing my work, researching possible markets, sending out manuscripts, making follow-up phone calls, and on, and on?

Tricks of the Trade

Reading Logs and Journals
       Keep It Simple
       The Daily Reading Log
       The Detail/Event Log
       The Double-Entry Journal
       The Guided Response

The Reading Questionnaire
       The Theory
       The Practice

Shared Journal Writings
Possible Journal Topics
Be Prepared for Book Challenges
Book Completion Form
Book Recommendation Card
Mandated Reporting of Known or Suspected Child Abuse
Resources and Hotlines for Youth and Their Allies
Simple Ways to Encourage a Reading Habit
The SAFARI Program
Mirrors of the Soul—Windows to Others
Simple Ways to *Discourage* a Reading Habit
Getting Help for Troubled Students

Reading Logs and Journals

Keep It Simple

The Theory: If a major teaching goal is to give students the gift of a lifetime reading habit, then we need to reinforce skills that will carry over into their adult lives. When we read for pleasure as adults, we read freely, without the burden of anticipated book reports. When we've finished our book, we don't go to the computer and take a comprehension test. We don't track our progress in reading skills. We don't write a book report. We don't make a diorama of a scene from what we've just read. We don't redesign the cover. We probably talk with a friend or two about the book. If we really liked it, we may go to the library or the bookstore to find more books by the same author. We may discuss the book in a book group. If we're journal keepers, we may write about the book in our journals. But we do that because it serves our own purposes.

Dioramas have their place in language arts classrooms, as do other art projects related to books. Readers Theatre is a great activity for enhancing understanding and enjoying a text. Role-playing characters, using charts to help students organize comparison/contrast essays, writing a story in the style of the author just read—all of these can be great motivators. But none of them does much to encourage a lifelong independent reading habit. Such activities should be supplemental and should not take time away from scheduled SSR.

Purists claim that classes designed to develop independent readers should include plenty of silent reading time. The only other activities that should take place in the SSR program are those that support a community of readers. Booktalks, occasional reading aloud, and spontaneous discussion regarding books being read are all appropriate, and these are things adult readers often experience.

The purist's stance is that book reports, log sheets, comprehension checks, anything that doesn't translate to a life-after-school reading habit should be off limits. This idea makes sense in theory, and I'm sure there are some teachers who follow the purist line and do wonders to aid and abet lifelong reading. Most of us, though, are somewhat bound by a grade book and are expected to hold students accountable in one way or another. And, the truth is that many students like the security of keeping track of their progress. From my point of view, a simple Reading Log is a useful tool in the SSR classroom, even though it doesn't meet the criteria of carrying over into adult reading habits.

Book reports are another story. Some students are so lacking in writing proficiency that the thought of completing a book report makes them want to feign illness and stay home from school indefinitely. This lack of proficiency is a problem, but it's not a problem to be solved, or even addressed, in a Sustained Silent Reading program. Significant reading time will eventually help the poor writer, but taking the joy out of reading by adding the burden of a book report is counterproductive. If any requirement takes significant time away from reading time, dump it.

The Daily Reading Log

The Daily Reading Log is the simplest form of log, with an estimated time of completion of about one minute. Even the least proficient writers can successfully maintain this record with a minimum degree of anxiety.

The Detail/Event Log

The Detail/Event Log asks that students write one detail or event from their reading and give that day's reading an interest rating. This offers a useful record and the daily ratings help you know whether it's time to guide the reader to a different book. The estimated time of completion using this form ranges from one minute to five or more for less-proficient writers. For those students who struggle to write, even this simple form can border on drudgery.

The Double-Entry Journal

The Double-Entry Journal type of Reading Log asks students to copy a quotation from the day's reading and then to write something about the passage they've chosen. The estimated time of completion here is up to five minutes for the more proficient writers, and way too long for the strugglers.

The Guided Response

The Guided Response Reading Log is even more demanding because it calls for abstractions. In a class of resistant, low-level learners, the estimated time of completion for this log is somewhere between ten minutes and eternity. It isn't a log that fits very well into the reading-for-real category. I've included it mainly because this type of log can be a useful guide in your informal, one-on-one conversations with readers. And, that *does* fit into a reading-for-real classroom.

The Daily Reading Log

Name _____

Date	Title of Book	Pages Read

The Detail/Event Log

Name of Student _____

Book Title	Date	Pages Read	Detail/Event from Reading	On a 1–10 scale, rate your interest in today's reading
Example: *Love Rules*	5/22/05	98–102	Conan and Lynn are pulled over by sheriffs	9

Double-Entry Journal

Name _____   Title _____

Date	Quotation	**Response:** Write any thoughts, questions, predictions, or whatever comes to your mind as you consider the passage.

Guided Response Reading Log

What I know so far about the story is . . .	What I've learned so far about the main character(s) is . . .	What I've learned about myself by reading this is . . .	What I've learned about my reading is . . .

The Reading Questionnaire

The Theory

Here's another suspect "reading for life" activity. When is the last time you filled out a questionnaire before getting down to the business of reading a book? Well . . . But . . .

Here's what's good about the questionnaire. It establishes an attitude of respect for the reader. It shows that you value your student's own perceptions and insights. It offers the student a sense that his/her ideas and opinions are important.

The Practice

The questionnaire offers an easy introduction to a new student. You may work in a setting with an ever-changing enrollment of at-risk students. Students are removed from your rolls because they've moved, or got a job during school hours, or been arrested, or . . . New students show up who've recently moved to your district, or been kicked out of the "big" high school, or been released from juvenile hall. After the new kid arrives, have him fill out the questionnaire. During reading time, sit with him and talk about his answers. If he hates to read, assure him that you will work diligently to help him find something of interest. Based on his answers about what he might like to read, or what movies he likes, offer a couple of books that might be a fit. Assure him they are not assigned, but only suggestions.

The Reading Questionnaire offers important information. Even though she rates her reading skills as average, but her test scores show her to be way below average, her attitude and sense of confidence is a significant factor in her approach to reading. If he says he needs help with comprehension, or any other specific skill, this is a good time to reassure him that he can greatly improve these skills in the reading classroom. And, it offers an opening for you to spend five minutes or so before silent reading time to give a quick lesson in one of the areas of desired improvement.

As an example of a quick lesson in a needed skill, a teacher might say, "I notice on the questionnaires that several of you want to increase your reading speed. One helpful technique is to underline what you're reading with your index finger. Guide your eye just slightly faster than is comfortable. This simple action can increase your reading speed by 30 percent." Demonstrate the underlining technique. Suggest that students practice the technique during silent reading. Model the behavior.

The Reading Questionnaire can serve as a guidepost to harken back to. Check with the students after a month or so to see if their answers remain the same, or if some things have changed.

For a host of other specific techniques for struggling readers, see *When Kids Can't Read What Teachers Can Do* by Kylene Beers and *Reading Reminders—Tools, Tips and Techniques* by Jim Burke.

Reading Questionnaire

Name _____   Date _____

Teacher _____   Period _____

In your opinion, are your reading skills: good   average   poor

List any books you've read and liked in your lifetime:

Which magazines or newspapers do you like to read?

List any subjects you might like to read about:

Which movies have you liked the most?

Which TV programs do you like to watch?

What are you presently reading during silent reading time or on your own time?

Is the book you're reading holding your interest?

What other book(s) might you like to read?

What areas, if any, do you need help with (word recognition, comprehension, increasing reading speed, concentration, etc.)? Please explain.

Other comments? (Please use the back of the paper if you need more room.)

Shared Journal Writings

My essay, "Youthful Recklessness," published in *English Journal*, January 1996, explains and reflects on the process of shared journal writings between teachers and students.

Youthful Recklessness

One of my practices as a high school English teacher has long been to ask students to write on a topic of their own choosing, from their own experiences. Knowing some will blank out over a topic choice, I prime the pump with a list of suggestions: What is something you will never forget? Write about a time when things were going well for you. Where in your life do you feel safe and at peace? Write from the heart, I advise them, knowing how difficult it is for many of them to express what is in their young, burdened hearts. I return their papers within a day or two, with comments about their ideas and experiences.

Once a week, or so, we reverse the process. I choose a topic from the list and write from my own aging heart. Thanks to the miracle of photocopying machines, I am able to give each student a copy of my writing, which they then read and write comments on. Some of the more vocal cannot limit their comments to the written word. One girl, particularly, will linger in my memory after others fade. Sandra would consistently blurt out her own strongly held opinions regarding whatever piece of my life I'd chosen to reveal. Sometimes she was sympathetic, sometimes scornful, but always quick to make her views known.

Awhile back, several students chose to write about a time when they suffered some sort of physical injury. Most wrote of the usual sports mishaps and childhood falls, but a few had more dramatic and frightening stories to tell. One had been hit by a car and would forever walk with a severe limp. Sheila wrote of a time when she was "still a kid" and had been jumped by a gang of older girls. Another student had been stabbed by a rival gang member. One confessed that his mother had beaten him regularly for several years, until he was placed in a foster home. Their writings got me thinking about the dangers of being young. In some ways, my students' dangers were much greater than mine had been, and in some ways not. I decided that I would write to them about a time I was injured, even though it meant confessing to behavior unbecoming a future teacher.

The time was 1952, when I was seventeen, I wrote. It was a clear, brisk, spring morning, and my two best girlfriends, Bobbie and Shirley, and I, had cut class. We were in Bobbie's 1932 Ford convertible, driving around in the foothills, smoking Pall Mall cigarettes and talking about boys.

Bobbie and Shirley began to sing, "Got Along Without You Before I Met You, Gonna Get Along Without You Now." They asked me to sing, too, but I didn't want to. We argued, jokingly, and then Bobbie stopped the car and told me to either sing or get out. I got out. We were all laughing. Shirley closed the door and Bobbie started to drive away.

We were miles from a phone, or a bus stop. When the car pulled away, I jumped on the *running board* (check your dictionaries or ask your grandparents for the meaning of this term), but there was nothing really to hold on to. I balanced precariously, leaning into the canvas top, but the faster we went, the worse it got. I pounded on the windshield and screamed, "I can't hold on!" Bobbie panicked and, instead of slowing gradually from her thirty mile per hour speed, she slammed on the brakes. My body was impelled forward, toward the fender, toward the asphalt, ahead of the skidding car. I pushed off the side of the car and went sprawling into the gutter, feeling the swish of wind as the back wheel barely cleared my leg. I slid, fast, gathering asphalt and abrasions along the way. My friends came running back to me, screaming and crying. I managed to lift my head and say, "I'm not singing. You can't make me." We laughed, hysterically, then got back in the car and went to Shirley's house where we drank her father's whiskey and put our minimal knowledge of first aid to use.

My hands, elbows, and knees were bloodied. Even the tip of my nose was skinned. There was a perfectly round hole in my skirt, slip, and underpants, where my pelvic bone and the asphalt had met. Beneath the hole in my clothing was a nasty raw spot. When I got home, my mother wanted to know what happened. I told her I had fallen at school, running across the quad. She became alarmed when she saw what was under my torn clothing and took me to the doctor. He dressed my wounds and asked my mother to leave us alone.

"Do you want to tell me what really happened?" he asked. I shook my head no. "Then tell me, when you hit the pavement, how fast were you running?"

"About thirty miles an hour," I admitted.

"Talk to the track coach," he said, patting me on the back and helping me ease down from the examining table.

I was very sore for a week or so, and I've never again jumped on a moving vehicle. But when I think back to that time of youthful recklessness, I think of all I would have missed if I'd gone over the fender and under the wheel instead of off to the side of the road, and I thank the Grand Goddess of the Harmonic Universe for sparing my life.

Here are some things I would never have experienced: The joy of a true and lasting love. The beauty of lightning reflected off glacial peaks in the Swiss Alps. The pleasure, pain, and laughter that goes with life at Misunderstood High School. The flooding of love for the innocent infant daughters and son whose lives depended on me. The accomplishment of putting myself through college after wasting my high school opportunities. Seeing my first published essay in a major national newspaper, and then, my first published book. Swimming in the clear, warm waters of the Caribbean. And so much more.

My hope for each of you, I wrote to my students, is that you will live your lives in such a way as to stay clear of danger, and that you will not die young, of stupidity, as I nearly did. I hope that you will live through your time of youthful recklessness, and grow to value yourselves, and to treat yourselves with care, so that you may enjoy the fullness of life, and all the coming years hold in store for you.

I wrote this to them, knowing that just as the words of my parents and teachers did not keep me off that long ago running board, my words were no match for their youthful, thoughtless impulsiveness.

Not long ago, Sheila, who had commented on my account of the running board caper by telling me, and the whole class, what an idiot I had been and how lucky I was to still be alive, attempted to run across the freeway to help a friend whose car was broken down. In that one reckless act, she lost her life.

In my classes I continue to extol the importance of thinking before one acts, of taking care of one's precious life. I know that is not the nature of youth. But I pray that their luck will hold, in a crucial moment, as mine did, rather than fail, as did Sheila's.

Possible Journal Topics

Choose from These When Your Mind Is Blank

Here are just a few of the endless possibilities for topics. It's best to only offer three choices, or journal writing time can be totally eaten up by choosing a topic. If it's not already included, a reminder to "explain in detail" should be added to each of these prompts.

1. Write three wishes and explain how your life would change if they came true.
2. Write about a time when you were very happy.
3. Write about a time when you were very sad.
4. Write about a time when you were very angry.
5. Write about a place where you feel totally safe.
6. Write three things about which you worry, and explain why.
7. Write about a nightmare. Give details.
8. Write in detail about your first memory.
9. Write about a time you wanted to, or did, run away. Explain fully.
10. Write ten statement pairs starting "I used to be _____, but now I'm _____."
11. Write ten statement pairs starting "I used to think _____, but now I know _____."
12. Write ten things you don't know, but wish you did. Is there anything you do know, but wish you didn't?
13. Write about a time when you felt particularly good about yourself.
14. Write about a time when you felt particularly bad about yourself.
15. Write about a time when a friend disappointed you.
16. If you could offer your father or mother one gift, not money, what would it be? How would it affect his or her life? (The gift may be material, or it could be something less tangible such as good health or a happy spirit.)
17. If you could change one thing about yourself, what would it be?
18. Write about a time when you did something nice for someone else.
19. Write about a favorite childhood memory.
20. Write about a very bad childhood memory.
21. Describe your life five years from now.
22. Describe your life forty years from now. (No fair being dead.)
23. Write about learning to ride a bicycle.
24. Write about a time when you were terribly frightened.
25. Write about a time when you felt loved.
26. Write about a time when you were terribly embarrassed.

27. Write about a time when you felt picked on and put-down.
28. Describe the ideal school.
29. Describe the ideal friend.
30. Write about a time when you did something you later regretted.

Resources

Values Clarification, by Sidney B. Simon, Leland W. Howe, and Howard Kirschenbaum, is a treasure of thought-provoking questions that can easily be turned into journal prompts.

Journal Jumpstarts: Quick Topics and Tips for Journal Writing, by Patricia Woodward, is also a good source of ideas.

Be Prepared for Book Challenges

Book challenges come from all directions, with a variety of motives, though fear is at the very core of a need for repression. Organized campaigns against certain titles may come from the right and be vitriolic and widely publicized. Predictions of the ruination of the moral fiber of our youth can run rampant.

Occasionally challenges come from the other side, with an organization wanting a book removed from the shelf because of language interpreted as being degrading to a particular racial or ethnic group. Sometimes it is a lone parent, concerned that a certain book, or books, will lead innocent Johnny astray.

In "Planning Ahead for the Book Challenge That Is Sure to Come," Edna Boardman advises:

> A selection policy is your first line of defense. Think and plan right now about how you select your materials. Establish a written policy that includes a procedure for handling a materials challenge.

It is likely that your school board has a selection policy in place. Get a copy and familiarize yourself with it, and keep it on file. Usually the policy will include statements to the effect that materials are selected to implement the curriculum and are chosen by those who know the courses of study and the abilities of students. Often it is suggested that book choices be backed up by three or more positive reviews. Some policies, particularly related to library selections, include student requests as a criteria for procurement.

For your purposes as an SSR teacher searching for "hit" books, student requests should take priority, along with books from the Mirrors of the Soul—Windows to Others list (TOTT) and other book lists that consider reluctant readers. If you worry a lot, and if a title seems particularly vulnerable to challenges, go to the Amazon website and read the reviews to see if your book could meet the requirement of three or more positive reviews.

If for some reason your district has neglected to establish a selection policy, and your school doesn't have such a policy, write your own. Keep it simple. Share it with your principal and/or department head, and keep the policy on file with your records of book orders.

A possible book selection policy for SSR might state:

> *In order to pursue the goal of establishing a lifelong reading for pleasure habit, books will be selected with student interests, needs, and abilities in mind.*
>
> *Many of these books will be chosen from recommended lists put out by the American Library Association and other respected educators.*

Three or more positive published reviews will exist for titles where such reviews are available.

In addition to a written selection policy, you'll want to be sure that a policy exists regarding a Request for Reconsideration procedure. This is crucial to ensuring a reasonable process. Again, most school districts have these in place. If your school administration is not aware of such a "first step" form, check with your librarian. He or she likely has one or can find one for you. Here is a sample of a Request for Reconsideration:

> *When the principal, librarian, or teacher receives a complaint, the complainant will be asked to complete a Request for Reconsideration form for the book and return it to the principal of the school.*
>
> *During the time of consideration, the questioned material will not be removed from the library or from circulation.*
>
> *A steering committee should be composed of two other school faculty members (e.g., the teacher responsible for selecting the material and a librarian or media director), the curriculum chairman, the complainant, and the principal. This committee will meet to discuss the reconsideration request and material in question.*
>
> *If the problem is not resolved through the steering committee, the committee may select a reviewing committee of at least three teachers, especially competent in the questioned field, competent laypersons, and a district representative. A secretary will record the entire order of business. If the parties are unable to reach an agreement, the difficulty will be resolved through the district's Board of Trustees.*

If the samples here are not right for you, consider other possibilities. Again, Edna Broadman offers helpful information:

> There is no need to invent your own from scratch. Common structure, phrasing, and contents of such policies are used across the profession and are available in books published by the American Library Association (ALA). The ALA's Intellectual Freedom Manual . . . is full of rationales hammered out as a result of real-life experiences. . . . The ALA's position is that there should be no age barriers to reading.

Ms. Broadman also highly recommends Henry Reichman's *Censorship and Selection: Issues and Answers for Schools.*

Chances are you will never be challenged, but if you are, stay cool. Keep a record of all contacts with the challengers. This is helpful in the event they try to misconstrue any interactions. Enlist the support of reasonable colleagues.

Ms. Broadman echoes my opinion when she states: "If you try to eliminate from you collection any materials to which someone might possibly object, you have your work cut out for you." She illustrates the difficulty of having objectionable free materials with this example:

> In a speech quoted in the September 1993 issue of "Newsletter on Intellectual Freedom (ALA)," Joan Delfattore, author of *What Johnny Shouldn't Read: Textbook Censorship in America*, tells of a California law that forbids schools to promote non-nutritious food. Result: The short story "A Perfect Day for Ice Cream" became "A Perfect Day," and a scene set in an ice cream parlor was neatly excised. Censorship takes an almost infinite number of forms.

Don't let yourself be intimidated by the possibilities of challenges. Most often challenges are resolved quickly and books stay on shelves. Even if you find yourself on the losing end of a heated battle and are compelled to remove a book, you end up being a hero to the vast majority of your students and their parents. Don't sell your readers short because of something that may never happen. Don't avoid "hit" books out of fear. Stay with the brave choices that have meaning for your readers. If you need help, there are many places to turn; here are a few:

National Coalition Against Censorship, 275 Seventh Avenue, New York, NY, 10001, 212-807-6222—*ncac@netcom.com, www.ncac.org.*

Office for Intellectual Freedom, American Library Association, 50 East Huron Street, Chicago, IL 60611, 800-545-2433, ext. 4222—*jkrug@ala.org, www.ala.org/alaorg/oif/.html.*

The Freedom to Read Foundation—*www.ftrf.org.*

The American Civil Liberties Union—*www.aclu.org.*

People for the American Way, 2000 M Street NW, Suite 400, Washington, DC 20036, 202-467-4999—*www.pfaw.org.*

The National Coalition Against Censorship—*www.ncac.org.*

Book Completion Form

Here is another suspect "reading for life" activity. You probably don't fill out this type of form after you finish reading the latest literary novel or action/thriller. If your memory cells are falling by the wayside, as are mine, you might jot a few notes in your journal to help you remember the book, but it's a stretch to say a Book Completion Form is pertinent to a lifelong reading habit.

In spite of not exactly fitting the purist's SSR standards, this form gives you something to record in your class record book, and it helps you keep track of students' reading interests and progress. It is simple enough to not be difficult for most readers. Simply talk through the more abstract questions with those for whom filling out even this form will be seen as *burdensome*.

Book Completion Form

Name _____   Date _____

Teacher _____   Period _____

Book Title _____

Author _____ Copyright Year _____

On a scale of 1 to 10, 10 being best, please rate this book _____

What does this book say about life?

Do you agree or disagree with this view of life? Please explain briefly.

Which of the characters in this book are most like you? Explain.

Would you like to read more books by this author? _____

Extra Credit Possibilities

   Complete a Book Recommendation Card and place it in the Recommended
      Books file.
   Using the Book Recommendation Card as a guideline, give a brief booktalk to
      a small group of students, or to the whole class.

Book Recommendation Card

Although not exactly a "reading for life" activity, the Book Recommendation Card comes close. Those of us who are lifelong readers do recommend books to friends. Keeping a card file in the classroom with recommendations from students can be a useful tool for others to decide on books to read, and it is in keeping with "reading for life" standards.

Book Recommendation Card

Book Title _____   Rating (1–10) _____

Author _____

Fiction/Action Adventure _____   Young Adult _____   Literary _____

Sci-Fi _____   Mystery/Detective _____   Fantasy _____

Nonfiction Biography/Autobiography _____   Science _____   History _____

Nature _____   Psychology _____   Social Issues _____

Other category? _____

What did you most like about this book?

Why do you think others might like it?

Mandated Reporting of Known
or Suspected Child Abuse

There are several situations for which educators are mandated by law to report. One is child abuse; another is a threat by a student to harm himself or others, or otherwise commit a dangerous act.

If you are not now aware of your district's policies, it's a good idea to review them. Such situations are highly sensitive, and you want to be sure you handle them in the best possible way.

States and school districts vary in the details of how to deal with such reporting. For the sake of example, here's how it works in some school districts in California:

> Teachers must immediately report by telephone any known or reasonably suspected instance of abuse. You are not to wait until the end of the day, or your conference period, when it's convenient for you to make the call.

> In California, failure to report known or suspected cases of abuse is a misdemeanor with the possibility of six months in jail and a fine of up to $1,000 or both. Failure to report may also result in the loss of one's credential.

> In some districts teachers may report directly to a principal, counselor, nurse, or other support staff (e.g., as I did with Irma, discussed in Chapter 5). But *you* are still responsible to see that proper reports are made within the mandated time frame. If you believe the child to be in immediate danger, you are to call 911 for an immediate response. A written report must be made within thirty-six hours. A Suspected Child Abuse Form should be available at your school site. If not, pick one up from the Office of Child Welfare and Attendance.

Your district should, and probably does, provide you with a list of telephone numbers for reporting. These will likely include protective services offices and local police and sheriff's departments.

For the sake of clarification, Elk Grove School District, in California, defines child abuse as:

> Any act of commission or omission that endangers or impairs a child's physical or emotional health and development. Child abuse crosses all socio-economic, racial, religious, cultural, occupational, and ethnic boundaries. It is perpetrated by both men and women, and both boys and girls are victims.

They list and describe four categories of child abuse: physical abuse, sexual abuse and exploitation, emotional abuse and deprivation, neglect and/or inadequate supervision.

Your district will have guidelines regarding how to talk with a student who has revealed such problems to you. It's a good thing to stay calm and to reassure the student that you will try to get help for him or her. Let the student know that you have to report the incident and that someone may come to talk with him or her.

If you work with at-risk kids (and really, who doesn't?), there is a strong likelihood that you'll be faced with the necessity of filing a suspicion of abuse report somewhere along the way. It isn't fun. Students are likely to feel betrayed. They're frightened that someone they love will get in trouble. They're frightened that things will get even worse. You're probably frightened too.

In my own experience with Estelle (see Chapter 4), I dreaded the process, but when she finished *Telling* and said, "something like this happened to me once," I knew it had to be done. I took her into a conference room and told her I needed to report the information that she had been molested. She cried and begged me not to. It had happened a few years back in Mexico. It was her uncle and she never ever saw him anymore. But it would really upset her mother if she found out, and her mother had heart problems, and really everything was fine now. I again explained that I was compelled to report her previous molestation, and reassured her that I would stay with her during the interview to help her explain about her mother.

A few hours later, a woman from Protective Services came to talk with Estelle. She insisted on also talking with the mother, which she did that evening. The mother *was* upset, but she rose to the occasion and was understanding and supportive of Estelle. Through the school, we managed to get short-term counseling for them—something to which they both easily agreed.

Things worked out well for Estelle and I was greatly relieved. I've seen it go the other way, when a student who is being molested by a stepfather is taken from her home and placed in foster care away from her mom, sisters, friends, and away from a school in which she was doing well. Why does the misused lose her home and the abuser gets to stay? That's another of those three A.M. questions.

Journals are a place where confidences are often offered. On a weekly basis I reminded my students that if they wrote about being abused, or wanting to commit suicide, or planning to kill a boyfriend or girlfriend who had wronged them, I would have to report such revelations to someone who could do more about their situation than I could. Nevertheless, I encouraged them to "write from the heart." When I got the rare reportable information, I saw it as a plea for help and set the wheels in motion, while at the same time I tried to be a source of support to the student now caught in the system. It's never easy.

Resources and Hotlines for Youth and Their Allies

Speaking of journals, what if a student writes that she suspects she is pregnant and is frightened and confused? She hasn't told anyone yet. You are not mandated to do anything with this information. And it's more than likely out of your realm of expertise to counsel her. But your heart goes out to her and you know she needs help. It's a good idea to *write* back to her in her journal, telling her that you're concerned. Give her a teen pregnancy hotline number, and ask if she wants help.

There are all kinds of unspoken, unwritten troubles that your students are struggling with and of which you are blissfully unaware. Keep an easy-to-read list of hotlines posted in an easily accessible place. The following numbers are national, but it's also good to include local numbers; your school counselor should be able to supply that information.

Abortion

Planned Parenthood provides family planning information, educational information, and referrals, in addition to health centers that provide contraception and abortion. All Planned Parenthood health centers provide confidential services to teens.

> Planned Parenthood Health Center Locator
> 24 hours a day, 7 days a week
> 800-230-PLAN (800-230-7526)

National Abortion Federation Hotline offers factual information about pregnancy options and abortions in both Spanish and English; confidential, nonjudgmental support; referrals to qualified abortion providers in the caller's area; referrals to funding sources; case management for women in difficult situations.

> 9 A.M.–7 P.M. EST, Monday-Friday; 9 A.M.–3 P.M. EST, Saturday
> 800-772-9100

Domestic Violence

National Domestic Violence Hotline counselors offer help in Spanish and English to victims of domestic violence. The staff provides information, referrals, and crisis intervention for men and women dealing with domestic violence.

> 24 hours a day, 7 days a week
> 800-799-SAFE (800-799-7233)
> 800-787-3224 TTY

Eating Disorders

National Eating Disorders Association hotline offers information and treatment referral for anyone having questions about eating disorders.

> 800-931-2237

Gay, Lesbian, Bisexual, Transgender Youth

The Gay and Lesbian National Hotline—Volunteer-run organization and hotline. Offers nonjudgmental support to anyone with questions about gay, lesbian, bisexual, or transgender sexuality. Refers callers to local service organizations and relays safe sex information in relation to HIV.

> Monday–Friday, 4 P.M. to midnight EST
> Saturday 12 P.M.–5 P.M. EST
> 888-THE-GLNH (888-843-4564)

Trevor Hotline—Crisis intervention and suicide prevention for gay, lesbian, bisexual, transgender, and questioning youth.

> 24 hours a day, 7 days a week
> 800-850-8078

The Gay and Lesbian Victims' Assistance Hotline is answered by trained volunteers who provide information and referrals to persons who have experienced violence or more common anti-gay incidents, such as discrimination, harassment, or vandalism. Callers may remain anonymous and all information is kept strictly confidential.

> 24 hours a day, 7 days a week
> 800-259-1536

Rape, Incest, Sexual Assault

The Rape, Abuse and Incest National Network (RAINN) is the nation's largest antisexual assault organization. RAINN operates the National Sexual Assault Hotline and carries out programs to prevent sexual assault, help victims, and ensure that rapists are brought to justice. Help is free and confidential.

> 24 hours a day, 7 days a week
> 800-656-HOPE (800-656-4673)

Runaway/Homeless

Covenant House offers residential and nonresidential help and services to homeless and runaway youth. Residential help includes food, shelter, clothing, and crisis care. Nonresidential help, through the hotline, offers referrals and emotional support for youth, parents, or families in crisis. Services are free and confidential.

> 24 hours a day, 7 days a week
> 800-999-9999

Sexually Transmitted Diseases/HIV/AIDS

Teens Teaching AIDS Prevention (TEENS T.A.P.)—A national hotline founded by teens for teens to provide education and information to other teens across the United States about how to prevent the transmission of HIV, the virus that causes AIDS. Teens staff the toll-free hotline to answer questions.

> 800-234-TEEN
> 800-234-8336
> M–F, 4:00 P.M.–8:00 P.M. (Central Time)

Center for Disease Control National STD and AIDS Hotline staff answer questions about prevention, risk, testing, treatment, and other STD, HIV, and AIDS-related concerns; it provides referrals and sends free publications through email and postal mail.

> 24 hours, 7 days a week
> 800-342-2437

Center for Disease Control National STD and AIDS Hotline

> 24 hours a day, 7 days a week
> 800-243-7889 (TTY, for Deaf and Hard of Hearing)
> 800-344-7432 (Spanish)

Substance Abuse

Center for Substance Abuse Treatment Referral Helpline is run by US Department of Health and Human Services to assist people with substance abuse addictions. Counselors are available to offer emotional support and refer callers to local treatment centers.

> 24 hours a day, 7 days a week
> 800-662-4357

Alcoholics Anonymous (AA)—National organization with local affiliates throughout the United States and Canada. The primary purpose of organization is to help members get sober, maintain sobriety, and help other alcoholics achieve sobriety. Membership is free and confidential.

Check local phonebook for listings.

Alateen is a program affiliated with Alcoholics Anonymous to help young people whose lives have been affected by someone else's drinking.

8 A.M.–6 P.M. EST, Monday–Friday
888-4-AL-ANON (888-425-2666)

Suicide Prevention

National Hope Line Network phone assistance staffers offer emotional support and referrals. Instant referral to programs dealing with suicide prevention and counseling in caller's local area, including substance abuse and mental health services.

24 hours a day, 7 days a week
800-SUICIDE (800-784-2433)

Teen Pregnancy

Planned Parenthood provides family planning information, educational information and referrals in addition to health centers that provide contraception and abortion. All Planned Parenthood health centers provide confidential services to teens.

Planned Parenthood Health Center Locator
24 hours a day, 7 days a week
800-230-PLAN (800-230-7526)

Simple Ways to Encourage a Reading Habit

- Provide a wide variety of paperbacks—fiction, biography, horror, easy reading, and comeback stories, along with more complex and sophisticated material.
- Have students fill out a brief questionnaire about their reading interests, histories, and goals; use their responses in helping them find books that will capture their attention.
- Provide a comfortable, quiet place where students can, through books, sink into other worlds.
- Allow significant time for silent reading each day.
- Reassure readers that it's a good thing to change books if they lose interest in the ones they've first chosen.
- Read aloud from something funny, exciting, emotionally gripping.
- Pull up a chair and have each student read a paragraph, or so, to you. Talk with the student about what has just been read. Do this often enough so that it's not a big deal.
- Do booktalks on ten or so books, then leave them handy on a table for browsing.
- Emphasize the importance of reading. Use inspirational quotes from famous people regarding their reading habits. Remind students that by reading they are building vocabulary and language skills.
- Watch for materials that may be of interest to particular students—the loner, the gangbanger—"I thought this book might interest you, want to give it a try?"
- Have students make brief entries in a Reading Log after each reading session.
- Give five-minute reading suggestions relating to reading—comprehension, speed, phonics, literary terms, concentration.
- Model good reading behavior; share something about what you're reading.
- Encourage students to share a bit about what they are reading.
- Establish a community of readers, where students recommend, exchange, and discuss books.
- Recognize, reward, and publicize good reading practices.

Keep in mind that reading independently for one's own purposes is what keeps a reading habit alive and healthy long after school years have ended. If you can give a non-reader the gift of a lifelong reading habit, you've given the gift that goes on giving.

The SAFARI Program

Students
And
Faculty
All
Reading
Independently

Welcome to the SAFARI reading program. Each day, for 25 minutes, students and teachers read silently from books of their choice. Through the magic of reading, you can travel to fascinating places! Meet new people! Have hair-raising adventures! Gain insight into your own life and the lives of others!

Here's how to get on board the SAFARI expedition:

Choose a book that is of interest to you. If you have trouble finding something, your teacher will help you. (Sorry, magazines and newspapers are not appropriate SAFARI choices.)

Bring your book to fourth period every day. At the beginning of the class, open your book and start reading. Read silently for 25 minutes, then write a brief entry in your Reading Log. Your teacher will tell you when it is time to complete the log.

Change books if you don't like the book you've started. This is *your* journey, so make it interesting to *you*.

Share your reading experiences in occasional classroom discussion. Your teacher will periodically ask students to discuss their books. Let your classmates know if your book is worth reading. Listen to your classmates' talk about books to help you decide what to read next.

Remember, regular, independent reading improves your vocabulary, general reading skills, and writing skills. It will also help you pass the exams for graduation, obtain your GED certificate, or pass the test for an alternate diploma.

But wait! There's more. Reading enables you to better understand yourself and the world around you. A lifelong reading habit is a foundation for a successful and meaningful life. Wherever you are on the journey of life, keep reading!

Mirrors of the Soul—Windows to Others

Abuse, Rape

Anderson, Laurie Halse—*Speak*	Acquaintance rape
Crutcher, Chris—*Chinese Handcuffs, Whale Talk*	
Draper, Sharon M.—*Forged by Fire*	Abuse
Jean, Ferris—*Bad*	Girl in juvenile detention center
Flinn, Alex—*Breathing Underwater*	From the abusers viewpoint
Irwin, Hadly—*Abby My Love*	
Peck, Richard—*Are You in the House Alone*	
Pelzer, David—*A Child Called It*, etc.	Extreme family abuse
Reynolds, Marilyn—*Telling, Baby Help, But What About Me*	Molestation, rape, partner abuse
Sapphire, Ramona Lofton—*Push*	Family abuse, rape
Seabold, Alice—*The Lovely Bones, Lucky*	Rape, murder
Williams, Lori Aurelia—*Shayla's Double: Brown Baby Blues*	

Addiction

Anonymous—*Go Ask Alice*	Drugs, peer pressure
Gordon, Barbara—*I'm Dancing as Fast as I Can*	Prescription drugs
Green, Shep—*The Boy who Drank too Much*	Alcohol
Knapp, Caroline—*Drinking, a Love Story*	Alcohol
Winik, Marion—*First Comes Love*	Heroin addiction

Adoption

Duncan, Lois—*Stranger with My Face*
Kingsolver, Barbara—*The Bean Trees*
Smith, Cynthia Leitich—*Rain Is Not My Indian Name*

Bullying

Cormier, Robert—*The Rag and Bone Shop*
Howe, James—*Misfits*
Plum-Ucc, Carol—*The Body of Cristopher Creed*

Reynolds, Marilyn—*Love Rules*
White, Ruth—*Belle Prater's Boy*

Gay/Lesbian

Block, Francesca Lia—*Weetzie Bat, etc.*	Gay/quirky
Brown, Rita Mae—*Rubyfruit Jungle*	Lesbian/coming of age
Chbosky, Stephen—*The Perks of Being a Wallflower*	
Ferris, Jean—*Eight Seconds*	Gay/bullying
Garden, Nancy—*Annie on My Mind*	Lesbian experience
Homes, A. M.—*Jack*	Gay father
Kerr, M. E.—*Deliver Us from Evie, Hello I Lied*	Sexual orientation
Koertge, Ron—*Arizona Kid*	Gay uncle
Mastoon, Adam—*The Shared Heart*	LBG narratives/photos
Monette, Paul—*The Last Watch of the Night, Becoming a Man*	
Reynolds, Marilyn—*Love Rules*	H.S. lesbian comes out
Ryan, Sara—*Empress of the World*	Questioning sexuality
Sanchez, Alex—*Rainbow Boys*	Gay high school boys

Grief

Guest, Judith—*Ordinary People*
Hawes, Louise—*Rosie in the Present Tense*
McDaniels, Lurline—Assorted titles
Lowry, Lois—*Summer to Die*
Williams-Garcia, Rita—*Every Time a Rainbow Dies*

Mental Illness

Axline, Virginia M.—*Dibs in Search of Self*	Identity search
Greenberg, Joanne—*I Never Promised You a Rose Garden*	Schizophrenic
Hyland, Betty—*The Girl with the Crazy Brother*	
Kaysen, Susanna—*Girl Interrupted*	Institutionalization
McCormick, Patricia—*Cut*	Self-mutilation
Nolan, Han—*Dancing on the Edge*	
Schreiber, Flora Rheta—*Sybil*	Multiple personality
Spungeon, Deborah—*And I Don't Want to Live This Life*	Manic, drugs

Sones, Sonya—*Stop Pretending: What Happened When My Big Sister Went Crazy*

Stoehr, Shelley—*Crosses Weird on the Outside*   Self-mutilation

Physical Handicaps

Bloor, Edward—*Tangerine*   Visually impaired

Crutcher, Chris—*Staying Fat for Sarah Byrnes*   Disfigured by burns

Dominick, Andi—*Needles: A Memoir of Growing up with Diabetes*

Grealy, Lucy—*Autobiography of a Face*   Disfigured by cancer

Laird, Elizabeth—*Loving Ben*   Hydrocephalic baby

Lewis, Catherine—*Postcards to Father Abraham*   Leg lost to cancer

Philbrick, Rodman—*Freak the Mighty*   Small, disfigured

Taylor, Theodore—*The Weirdo*   Scarred face

Trueman, Terry—*Stuck in Neutral*   Profound Cerebral Palsy

Voight, Cynthia—*Izzy Willy Nilly*   Amputated leg

White, Ryan—*Ryan White, My Own Story*   AIDS

Racial/Ethnic Awareness

Anaya, Rudolfo A.—*Bless Me, Ultima*   Mexican American

Angelou, Maya—*I Know Why the Caged Bird Sings*   African American

Borland, Hal—*When Legends Die*   Native American–Ute

Brown, Clalude—*Manchild in the Promised Land*   African American

Cisneros, Sandra—*The House on Mango Street*, etc.   Mexican American

Clinton, Cathryn—*A Stone in My Hand*   Palestinian

Creech, Sharon—*Walk Two Moons*   Native American

Crutcher, Chris—*Whale Talk*   African American

Ellis, Deborah—*Breadwinner, Parvana's Journey*   Afghanistan/Taliban

Frank, Anne—*The Diary of Anne Frank*   Jewish

Grimes, Nikki—*Bronx Masquerade*   Multicultural

Haley, Alex—*The Autobiography of Malcolm X*   African American

Hidier, Tanuja—*Born Confused*   Native American

Ji-Li Jiang—*Red Scarf Girls: A Memoir of the Cultural Revolution*   Chinese

Laird, Elizabeth—*Kiss the Dust*   Kurdish refugee family

Lee, Harper—*To Kill a Mockingbird*   African American

Martel, Yann—*The Life of Pi*   Indian
(Hinduism/Christianity/Islam)

McCall, Nathan—*Makes Me Wanna Holler*   African American

McCourt, Frank—*Angela's Ashes*   Irish American

Miklowitz, Gloria—*Masada, The Enemy Has a Face*   Jewish

Mori, Kyoko—*Shizuko's Daughter*   Japanese

Morrison, Toni—*The Bluest Eye*   African American

Myers, Walter Dean—*Bad Boy: A Memoir*   African American

Reynolds, Marilyn—*Beyond Dreams*   Vietnamese American

Reynolds, Marilyn—*If You Loved Me*   Mixed race

Rodriguez, Luis—*Always Running*   Mexican American

Shakur, Tupak—*The Rose that Grew in Concrete*   African American

Sitomer, Alan Lawrence—*The Hoopster*   African American

Soto, Gary—*Local News, Buried Onions, etc.*   Mexican American

Staples, Suzanne Fisher—*Daughter of the Wind*   Pakistan

Tan, Amy—*The Joy Luck Club*   Chinese American

Wakatsuki Houston, Jeanne—*Farewell to Manzanar*   Japanese American

Walker, Alice—*The Color Purple*   African American

Weisel, Elie—*Dawn, Night*   Jewish

Whelan, Gloria—*The Homeless Bird*   Indian

Williams-Garcia—*Like Sisters on the Homefront*   Cuban

Wright, Richard—*Black Boy*   African American

Suicide

Miklowitz, Gloria—*Close to the Edge*

Morris, Winifred—*Dancer in the Mirror*

Peck, Richard—*Remembering the Good Times*

Pevsner, Stella—*How Could You Do It Dianne*

Picoult, Jodi—*The Pact: A Love Story*

Teen Pregnancy/Parenting

Anonymous (Beatrice Sparks)—*Annie's Baby: The Diary of a Pregnant Teen*

Klein, Norma—*No More Saturday Nights*

Morning Glory Press—*Teen Dads, Your Pregnancy and Newborn Journey, Nurturing Your Newborn, etc.*

Reynolds, Marilyn—*Detour for Emmy, Too Soon for Jeff, Baby Help*

Woolf, Virginia Euwer—*Make Lemonade*

Other Good Reads

Anderson, M. T.—*Feed*	SciFi
Benchley, Peter—*Jaws*	Horror
Brooke, Michael—*The Concrete Wave: History of Skateboarding*	
The Buford High School Series, Townsend Press	Contemporary problems, *easy* reading
Canfield, Jack—*Chicken Soup for the Teenage Soul*	Inspirational
Clancy, Tom—various	
Filipović, Zlata—*The Freedom Writers Diary*	Gangs, urban violence, etc.
Fleischman, Paul—*Seedfolks*	Short stories
Frank, E. R.—*Life Is Funny, America*	
Gallo, Don (ed.)—*On the Fringe*	Short stories—outsiders
Grisham, John—various	
Franco, Betsy (ed.)—*You Hear Me?, Things I Have to Tell You*	Teen writers
Hendrix, Jimmy—*'Scuse Me While I Kiss the Sky*	Autobiography
Hinton, S. E.—*The Outsiders, That Was Then, This Is Now*, etc.	Gangs, drugs, poverty
Hopkins, Jerry, et al.—*No One Here Gets Out Alive*	John Morrison
King, Stephen—various	
Klass, David—*You Don't Know Me, California Blue, Danger Zone, Home of the Braves*	
Koontz, Dean—various	
Koertge, Ron—*Stoner and Spaz*	Drugs, cerebral palsy
Miller, Frances A.—*The Truth Trap*	Gripping mystery
Notaro, Laurie—*The Idiot Girls' Action Adventure Club*	Quirky personal essays
Myers, Walter Dean—*Handbook for Boys, Monster*	
Oates, Joyce Carol—*Big Mouth and Ugly Girl*	Outsiders
Paulsen, Gary—*Hatchet, Eastern Sun, Winter Moon*	Coming of age
Peck, Robert Newton—*A Day No Pigs Would Die*	
Pike, Christopher—various	Scary
Ritter, John H.—*Choosing Up Sides, Over the Wall*	Sports
Souljah, Sister—*The Coldest Winter Ever*	Inspirational
Steele, Danielle—various	
Vonnegut, Kurt—*Breakfast of Champions*	

Wolff, Tobias—*This Boy's Life*	Coming of age autobiography
Woodward, Fred (ed.)—*Rolling Stone Images of Rock and Roll*	Music, nonfiction

Sources for Books of Interest to Teens

School librarians have a wealth of information about titles that are popular with teens. They are also usually eager to come into your classroom and do booktalks. Public librarians are also good sources, particularly if your library has a YALSA (Young Adult Library Services Association) librarian on its staff.

The following organizations offer recommendations of the newest and best of YA publications:

American Library Association (YALSA)—*www.ala.org/YALSA*

American Association of School Librarians—annual lists: Best Books for Young Adults, Quick Picks for Reluctant Readers, Popular Paperbacks for Young Adults, etc.

The ALAN Review, 209 MCH, Florida State University, Tallahassee, FL 32306-4490—*http://english.byu.edu/ALAN; http://scholar.lib.vt.edu/ejournal/alan-review.html*

Signal (Special Interest Group—a Network on Adolescent Literature), an International Reading Association publication; contact kellyp@vt.edu

English Journal—monthly Young Adult Literature column

Simple Ways to Discourage a Reading Habit

First, a confession: In my trial-and-error period of teaching, I probably used nearly all of these discouraging strategies at one time or another, with the exception of writing personal checks during SSR. But I thought about it, so, like Jimmy Carter, I sinned in my heart. If you recognize yourself in some of the following no-nos, grab the beverage of your choice and kick back in your lounger. Remind yourself of what a good person you are, a hardworking, conscientious teacher, doing your part to make things better. So you make a few mistakes along the way. So you're not perfect. But you're good, and the world is better off for the likes of you. Pat yourself on the back, but not so hard you'll have to see the chiropractor.

One more thing before you read the list: You have your own individual teaching style and you and everyone else must respect that. If you absolutely have to keep books safe in that locked cabinet, unlocking it only during certain times of SSR, do it. Work with it. The same thing goes for the books list. If there's a title on there that you are certain would be the undoing of the youth of America, skip it. You are the final authority in your classroom, and you must, with careful consideration, follow the pure light within you, and teach in accordance.

And now . . .

How to Discourage a Reading Habit

○ Provide only books that you deem to be worthy of reading, books which are recognized as quality literature, or which are morally uplifting.
○ Keep the most popular books in a locked cabinet so that they don't get lost.
○ Use SSR time to get caught up: grade papers, work on accreditation reports, write a few checks if you need to.
○ Become so involved in your own reading that you forget to notice who in your classroom is not involved in reading.
○ Rather than confront, allow a few students to talk all through SSR time.
○ To build responsibility, demand that students bring books to class every day. Don't keep a supply of interesting books on your shelves for those who forget to bring books to read during SSR. Let them sit and stare at the wall—no credit for the day. Remind them that it's time they grow up.
○ Demand good reading posture. Don't let them sit with books in their laps, head resting on the edge of the desk, or leaned way back with their books at arm's length.
○ Don't allow any spontaneous discussion of books from interested readers.
○ If a student says reading is boring and refuses to read during SSR, give him worksheets to keep him quiet.

○ Never, ever allow a student to read the same book twice.

○ Demand lengthy and academically challenging book reports that ask for analyses of plot, theme, tone, character development, symbolism, rising and falling action, and so on.

○ If a student wants to change books, talk with her about the importance of finishing what she starts. Maybe now is the time to explain the meaning of the aphorism: "Don't change horses in midstream."

○ If a student asks for help in understanding a word or sentence, remind him that this is Sustained *Silent* Reading time.

○ Don't bring in new books or take the time to do booktalks. You're trying to develop a lifelong reading habit and sooner or later they'll have to figure out how to choose their own books.

○ If you need added classtime to prepare students for standardized testing, use SSR time.

○ Schedule SSR for fifteen minutes only on two or three days a week. Be sure the days are not consecutive.

○ Remind students that *you* are the one with the college degree, and *you* know much better than they what they should be reading.

○ Be a grump more than half of the time.

Getting Help for Troubled Students

We've all had them—students who for whatever reason were unreachable/unteachable. Let's say you awaken in the middle of the night to a vision of Laura, endlessly lost in checking her makeup while your other twenty-nine students listen attentively to your words of wisdom.

You wonder whether we're not missing something—the magic turn-around wand that's just beyond your reach. You've done all you know to do. You've carefully considered the information from Laura's questionnaire. You've established that she has the necessary basic reading skills to do well in SSR. You've had mini-conferences with her to see what you can do to help her earn credit in your class. You've read with her. Moved her to another desk. Presented her with a wide array of reading choices. All the while, Laura continues to check her mirror, not make eye contact, and not open the cover of a book. You're discouraged, angered, fighting a sense of failure. You've prayed the serenity prayer, all to no avail. Now is the time to call on resources beyond the classroom. Keep Laura informed of what you're doing.

Let her know that you'll do one or more of the following things because you want to help her be successful in school and you haven't been able to figure out how to do that on your own:

- ○ Call home and talk with Laura's parent or guardian. Start the conversation on a positive note, even if the only thing you can think to say is that Laura's makeup always looks nice. Ask if he/she has any ideas about what you might do to get Laura on track.
- ○ Check Laura's records to see if she has learning difficulties that might keep her from functioning well in your class.
- ○ Note any positive remarks you can glean from her previous teachers.
- ○ Talk with her other teachers to see if any of them have found the magic Laura wand, or even had an iota of success engaging her in learning.
- ○ Ask the nurse to do a health evaluation. Might she need glasses? Could she be on medication that gets in the way of the learning process?
- ○ Ask the counselor to talk with Laura to see what her perception is regarding her progress and participation in your class. Is there something going on in Laura's life that makes it impossible for her to concentrate on reading? Do you remind her of the next-door neighbor who chased her down the street with a broom when she was five?
- ○ Ask that Laura be evaluated for possible placement in designated programs such as special ed.

○ Seek the help of your school or district psychologist. Of course, if yours is like most districts, there is one psychologist for 32,000 students, so it may take awhile. Fill out the request form anyway.

If, along the way in this process, nothing has changed, know that you've given it your best. If she's not disruptive, continue putting books on her desk as she continues putting makeup on her face, but devote your energies to students who will make progress. If she is disruptive, beg, plead, demand that she be removed from your class rolls.

Appendix A
How I Learned to Read

My earliest experience with school left me disappointed and disillusioned. The instant I returned home from my first day in kindergarten, I ran into the kitchen, picked up the *Los Angeles Times* from the breakfast table, scanned the front page, and began to wail.

"What in the world is the matter with you, Marilyn?" my mother asked.

I could only cry.

"Did the children pick on you at school?"

I shook my head no.

"Was the teacher cross with you?"

Another negative nod.

"What then?"

"I can't read," I sobbed.

"Don't be silly. Of course you can't read yet."

"But Daddy told me when I went to school I would learn to read. And I went to school, and I still can't even read the funny paper!"

When my father came home from his meat market that evening, he opened a cold bottle of Budweiser and poured some into a glass that had once contained pink pimento cheese. He sat the bottle in front of his place at the table, and the little glass in front of my place. But instead of joining him right away, as was my custom, I sat under the high ovened stove, next to Brownie.

"Come up here, Shug, and tell me about your first day at school."

I sat, looking at bits of sawdust stuck to a glob of grease on the sole of his shoe.

"Don't you want your beer?"

"You lied to me," I said. "You tell me not to lie but *you* lied to me."

His eyes flashed red as he grabbed me from under the oven and plunked me down in my chair in one swift move. He was a man who prided himself on his honesty and did not take kindly to being called a liar by his five-year-old daughter.

"I can't read the newspaper," I told him, beginning to cry again. I reminded him of his promise that I would learn to read when I went to school.

"Didn't they teach you anything today?" he asked incredulously.

"We played with big blocks and sang," I told him.

He shook his head. "What kind of school is that anyway?" he asked, looking in the direction of my mother who was peeling potatoes at the sink. She did not respond to his question.

Again my father shook his head. Then he picked up his Budweiser and walked into the living room. "I'll teach you to read," he said, reaching for a thin black book of Edgar A. Guest poems. I grabbed my beer glass and followed him.

We started with a poem called "Best Way to Read a Book" and my father explained that letters stood for sounds. He read a few words and then helped me puzzle one out and we went on that way, reading and drinking beer, until it was time for dinner. Now, upon rereading the poem, I see that it is sing-song and trite and sexist. But then it suited me just fine, and I felt better about playing at school, knowing that I was learning to read at home.

A few months later, the PTA sent out a bulletin on the pitfalls of parents attempting to help children learn to read. Different methods could lead to confusion, parents did not have special training, and so on, but it was too late then. I had begun to make sense of the printed word, and no one could stop me. From the names of the Dionne quintuplets pictured in the bottom of my cereal bowl, to the signs for Morrell Ham and Kraft cheese on the walls of my father's market, to the Buster Brown insignia inside my shoes—every understood word was a mystery unraveled and a sign of my own emancipation. Soon I could read the funny paper for myself and not have to wait for one of my parents to get around to it.

Appendix B
Nurturing Your Writing Self

Find a Writing Group

When I first started writing with intention, I wanted to eke out as much time for that task as possible. Why would I take a weekend to go to a writer's conference when I could be home writing? At times I begrudged the once-a-month Saturday morning meetings with the Pasadena group, time wasted eating, and talking about children, neighborhood disputes, husbands, religion, politics—sometimes hours and hours worth of chatter before we got to the real business of sharing manuscripts and critiques.

Eventually I became more enlightened. My view of the isolated writer expanded, not that there is no such thing as the isolated, hermitlike writer. That may be exactly what you need. But I came to realize that the interaction with other writers was of prime importance to my own development. Even the chitchat was important, though too much can kill a writing group.

A good place to find writers you might want to work with is through writing classes. Try an extension class at your local community college. If you meet a few people there whose work and comments you respect, talk with them about getting together when the class has ended.

Often bookstores sponsor writing groups. Drop in and see what's going on. It is crucial to find a writing group that fits your own particular needs. You will want a group that looks for what might make a manuscript better, rather than tearing it apart bit by bit and pointing out all major and minor errors. If you are only interested in writing science fiction, you might not want to stay with a group that consists mainly of writers working on children's books. If you happen into a group of mean-spirited critics, happen out.

Another way to meet with other writers is to get involved in your local branch of the National Writing Project. This has several advantages over other writing groups. It offers professional development. You can be fairly certain that the people you're working with are intelligent and responsible, and a major component of the project is that participants work on their own writing processes and products. Further information on this organization is available at *www.writingproject.org/*.

I hear from the more technically advanced that there are all kinds of writing groups and classes available on the Internet. Those you'll have to explore for yourself.

Get Tips, Laughs, and Inspiration from the Pros

Here's another idea I had to grow out of: Why would I take time away from my own writing to read about other writers?

Well, for one thing, most of them know a whole lot more than I do about the writing process and business. For another, it's stimulating and sometimes inspirational to sit with a writer, such as Eudora Welty, for an hour or so and drink in her perceptions and practices. Sometimes it's good for a laugh, and sometimes the practical information is exactly what's called for. There are seemingly as many books about writing as there are stars in the sky, but the following are a few of my favorites.

Anne Lamott's *Bird by Bird* is a wonderful book, thigh slappingly funny, honest, and practical; if I could recommend only one book, this would be it. Here's how much I love this book. At a conference awhile back I was talking about my books, particularly *Love Rules*. I encouraged people to come to my publisher's exhibit, where they could buy *Love Rules*, and other books in my series. I also sang the praises of *Bird by Bird*.

Afterward, I passed the sales booth that stocked *Bird by Bird*. Nearly everyone from my session was standing in line waiting to pay for that book. At the Morning Glory Press booth? Three people from that session bought *Love Rules*.

Stephen King, *On Writing*—I agree with amazon.com's statement that King "... gives you a whole writer's tool kit: a reading list, writing assignments, a corrected story, and nuts-and-bolts advice on dollars and cents, plot and character, the basic building block of the paragraph, and literary models."

Carolyn See, *Making a Literary Life—Advice for Writers and Other Dreamers*, is another wonderfully practical and funny book. See even goes so far as to put forth in detail the tax advantages available to writers, claiming that "your writing income ... offers you the opportunity to play a game that completely and legally rewards your creativity: Fun with the Tax Man."

Writers Market, published annually by Writer's Digest Books, is a tome. If you have back trouble and plan to buy the book, take along a friend to carry it out of the store for you. It's worth the effort though. According to the amazon.com review of the 2003 edition, "it includes invaluable listings of 1,400 consumer magazines, 450 trade magazines, 1,100 book publishers, and 200 script buyers, plus interviews with six freelance writers." There also are specifics on agents, cover/query letters; how to prepare a manuscript for mailing; listings for publishers that tell what kinds of works they're interested in, what they pay, how many books/articles they publish per year; and a wealth of other pertinent information.

Less practical, but certainly more literary, are Eudora Welty's *The Eye of the Story* and a book edited by Peggy Whitman Prenshaw, *Conversations with Eudora Welty*. Simply sinking into the clarity and richness of Eudora Welty's language must be good for any writer. I know it's good for me. Margaret Atwood, *Negotiating with the Dead—A Writer on Writing,* is a scholarly and highly literary piece of work; nevertheless, it is a very good read.

Frank Conroy edited *The Eleventh Draft,* which contains essays about writing by twenty-three contemporary writers, all once either students at the Iowa Writers' Workshop and/or on the faculty. This is a wonderfully varied collection, and nice to pick up for a quick read.

Virginia Woolf's *A Writer's Diary* is amazingly honest and unguarded; it is a vast understatement to describe it as "thought-provoking."

The Julia Cameron and Mark Bryan book, *The Artist's Way—A Spiritual Path to Higher Creativity,* is in a class all its own, a how-to when it comes to nurturing creativity. It is best experienced with a small group, working together through the prescribed twelve-step recovery program to free your creative spirit. In each step along the way, I could find something to fault—too didactic, sometimes arrogant, and sometimes schmaltzy—but working through this program was extremely valuable to me. If you only put into practice Cameron's plan for "Morning Pages" and the "Artist's Date," you will, I think, be surprised at how this stimulates the creative juices.

There are hundreds more books dealing with the art and craft of writing, but those mentioned here are well known to me, and I can recommend each of them with enthusiasm.

Appendix C
Down in Infamy

When I was very young—too young to know how old I was—I would sit on a high stool at a tall metal bathtub while Mama Okura washed vegetables and talked to me in a strange sing-song voice. Usually it was enough just to listen and watch her fast hands swishing the carrots and potatoes around under the water, tossing them onto a wooden counter, and reaching for more dirty vegetables from big gunny-sacks at her feet. One time though, I thought she wanted me to say something in response. She seemed to be trying to tell me something important. I thought it was about a bridge, or water, and I pretended to understand because I wanted to go back to the old way where she talked and washed and I watched and listened.

Mama and Papa Okura owned the produce section in the southern California store where my father had his meat market. There were six boys in the Okura family, ranging in age from around fifteen to twenty-six. (I can't be certain; because if I wasn't old enough to know my own age, I certainly wasn't old enough to know anyone else's.)

I could always understand the boys, but I could never understand what Papa Okura was saying. In fact, he hardly ever said anything to me. He did give me string beans to chew on, just as the rest of his family always did. I liked to watch him hose down and then sweep the cement floor at the front of the market, and I liked to watch him polish apples. His hands moved even faster than Mama Okura's did.

I especially liked the boys, and of them, I especially liked Ray. He would pick me up, ask a question, and then laugh. I liked how his eyes almost closed tight when he laughed.

Usually my parents referred to Mr. and Mrs. Okura as "Mama" and "Papa," but sometimes it was "the Japs," as in "You can't beat those Japs for hard work" or "Those Japs keep the prettiest produce sections in town," or other kinds of work-related compliments.

One Sunday, when I was six, I heard that "the Japs" had bombed Pearl Harbor. My mother was crying because her sister, my Aunt Hazel, lived near there. When my grandmother got to our house, she was crying too. There were a lot of telephone calls and neighbors dropping by and constant talk about bombs and Aunt Hazel.

That afternoon, we learned that Uncle Henry had been wounded at Hickam Field. People started talking about "those dirty Japs." I thought about the Okuras and the big metal bathtub, but I was afraid to ask any questions that day because I'd never seen my mother or grandmother cry before.

When Aunt Hazel came home, she cried a lot too. Uncle Henry had died from his wounds. They had been married three months.

One day when my aunt stopped by the market, Ray Okura told her he was sorry. I don't think she spoke to him, but I'm not sure because I only remember his face that day. I'd never seen him cry before, either.

Even before my aunt got back from Hawaii, Papa Okura had been taken away. He was accused of being a spy. My parents didn't think that was true, but, they said, you could never be sure in times of war.

It was not very many days after I saw Ray crying that the whole family was gone. Someone else, who didn't wash the vegetables in the big tub or give me string beans, had the produce department. He was okay, but I liked the Okuras better.

My mother and her friend, Willie, and I went one day to the internment camp at Santa Anita Racetrack to visit Mama Okura. The idea of staying in a camp sounded like fun. A lot of people were in the giant racetrack parking lot, living in tents and sitting on blankets under makeshift awnings. I wondered why they didn't seem to be having a good time.

My mother and Willie talked with Mama Okura for a while and left a package with her. She walked with us to the gate and cried when she said good-bye. I ran ahead to stop the Good Humor truck. I wanted an ice cream for her too. But when I turned to ask her what kind she wanted, she was slowly walking back to her tent. She didn't hear me call to her.

On the way home, I asked why the Okuras had left the market to live in the camp. Willie told me that they had to because of what "the Japs" had done at Pearl Harbor and Hickam Field. We had to protect ourselves from "bad Japs." It was hard for "good Japs" like Mama Okura and the boys. But we were at war now, and we had to be very careful and very strong.

In the late spring I planted a victory garden. I wanted string beans, but my mother told me they were too much trouble, so I planted carrots and radishes. I began saving tinfoil, and stamps to be turned into war bonds, and my father collected rendered fat at his market. All of these things were to help us win the war. I was sure we would beat "the Japs." I hardly ever thought about the Okuras, except sometimes when I passed the string bean bin at the market and wished that I could just reach out and take one without getting into trouble, and eat it right then, and know that it was clean. But I was growing up, and some things had already passed from my life forever.

Teachers Who Write

Ashton-Warner, Sylvia, *Teacher*
Codell, Esme Raji, *Educating Esme*
Coles, Robert, *The Call of Stories: Teaching and the Moral Imagination*
Conroy, Pat, *The Water is Wide*
Hayden, Torey L., *Somebody Else's Kids*
Herndon, James, *The Way it S'pozed to Be*
Herndon, James, *How to Survive in Your Native Land*
Johnson, Lou Anne, *Dangerous Minds*
Johnston, Michael, and Coles, Robert, *In the Deep Heart's Core*
Kaufman, Bel, *Up the Down Staircase*
Kozol, Jonathan, *Savage Inequalities*

Marilyn Reynolds' Realistic Fiction

True-to-Life Series from Hamilton High, Published by Morning Glory Press

Love Rules—". . . this is the best YA novel I have read with a central character who is gay—it is honest, explicit, complicated—all the characters are interesting and the issues are compelling." —Kliatt

If You Loved Me—"This is no sugar-coated fairy tale, but a gritty story where the ramifications of STDs, drug addiction and pregnancy are real and present . . . a great read with a moving lesson." —Today's Librarian

Baby Help—"An excellent YA novel with characters we care about." —Kliatt

But What About Me?—". . .the writing is superb and the realistic tone sets this book alongside the best of the genre . . . excellent addition to any YA collection" —School Library Journal

Too Soon for Jeff—". . . Jeff's world and relationships come alive . . . a thoughtful book for both young men and young women." —Booklist

Detour for Emmy—". . . wonderful novel . . . honest, heart-wrenching, informative . . . should be on all Best Books for YA lists." —Kliatt

Telling—"Sad, frightening, ultimately hopeful, and definitely a worthwhile purchase." —Booklist

Beyond Dreams—". . . book will hit home with teens." —Voya

Teaching guides are available for all of the above titles.

References

Works Cited

Abbot, Shirley. 1991. *The Bookmaker's Daughter: A Memory Unbound.* Boston, MA: Ticknor and Fields.

Beers, Kylene. 2003. *When Kids Can't Read, What Teachers Can Do: A Guide for Teachers 6–12.* Portsmouth, NH: Heinemann.

Bloom, Harold. 2001. *How to Read and Why.* Westport, CT: Touchstone Books.

Blume, Judy. 2001. *Places I Never Meant to Be.* NY: Aladdin Paperbacks.

Boardman, Edna M. 1994. "Planning Ahead for the Book Challenge That Is Sure To Come." *Library Talk: The Magazine for Elementary School* 7 (3): 17–18.

Burke, Jim. 2000. *Reading Reminders: Tools, Tips and Techniques.* Portsmouth, NH: Boynton/Cook.

The California Penal Code, Section 11172, Subdivision [e].

Delfattore, Joan. 1994. *What Johnny Shouldn't Read: Textbook Censorship in America.* New Haven, CT: Yale University Press.

Freedman, Samuel G. 1991. *Small Victories: The Real World of a Teacher, Her Students, and Their High School.* New York, Perennial.

Garden, Nancy. 2000. "A Writer's Perspective on Censorship." CSLA Journal: 23 (2): 17–18.

Humphrey's, Helen. 2001. *Afterimage.* New York: Metropolitan Books.

Lester, Julius. 2001. "Julius Lester on Censorship." In *Places I Never Meant to Be,* by Judy Blume. New York: Aladdin Paperbacks.

Mazer, Harry. 2001. "Harry Mazer on Censorship." In *Places I Never Meant to Be,* by Judy Blume. New York: Aladdin Paperbacks.

The National Resource Center on Child Sexual Abuse. 1994. "Fact Sheet on Child Sexual Abuse." Huntsville: NRCCSA

Pilgreen, Janice L. 2000. *The SSR Handbook.* Portsmouth, NH: Heinemann.

Reichman, Henry. 1993. *Censorship and Selection: Issues and Answers for Schools.* American Library Assn Editions; Revised edition: Chicago, IL.

Reynolds, Marilyn. 2001. *Love Rules.* Buena Park, CA: Morning Glory Press.

Schoemperlen, Diane. 2002. *Our Lady of the Lost and Found.* New York: Penguin

Simon, Sidney, Leland W. Howe, and Howard Kirschenbaum. 1995. *Values Clarification.* New York: Warner Books.

Temes, Peter. 2002. "Why Do We Read?" *Education Week* 21 (37).

Woodward, Patricia. 1996. *Journal Jumpstarts: Quick Topics and Tips for Journal Writing.* New York: Warner Books.

Woolf, Virginia. 1975. *The Common Reader: Second Series.* New York: Vintage/ Ebury (A Division of Random House Group).